Gerald Holtom

Designer of the Peace Symbol

Darius Holtom

SPOKESMAN

To my father

Published in 2022 by
Spokesman Books
5 Churchill Park
Nottingham, NG4 2HF
www.spokesmanbooks.org

Spokesman is the publishing imprint of the Bertrand Russell Peace Foundation Ltd.

ISBN 978 0 85124 9155

Contents

Introduction

I can remember my father, Gerald Holtom, running over Hythe beach with his bare feet crunching into the sharp shingle, then plunging into the cold, foamy breakers of the English Channel. He would emerge behind a wave and swim a relaxed front crawl, out to the flatter parts of the sea and the greener shades of grey where the water glistened with silver light. He was an artist who loved to immerse himself in the natural environment of *paradise earth,* as he used to say, which gave him an infinite source of inspiration.

Gerald Holtom lived through two world wars and the nuclear arms race during the Cold War. He was tormented by the thought that humanity and all the wonderful life forms that have come into being over millions of years of evolution, were now threatened by weapons of unimaginable destructive power. The image of his own father, shell-shocked and injured from the First World War, was also engraved in his mind. His thoughts on pacifism evolved through his education at Gresham's school and the Royal College of Art, which resulted in him becoming a conscientious objector in the Second World War. He was revolted by the atomic bombings of the two Japanese cities and found it intolerable that the H-bomb was still being developed; these events led to his involvement with the London to Aldermaston protest march against nuclear weapons in 1958, for which he designed the Unilateral Nuclear Disarmament Symbol, now known as the Peace Symbol.

I have put together my father's biography from his written memories, letters, family photographs and newspaper cuttings, which were left with me after he died in 1985. The biography traces his life as an artist, designer and peace activist. His works of art include some spectacular textile appliqué proscenium curtains that he made for schools, commissioned by the Ministry of Education. He also designed and built an innovative sailing craft with hydrofoils that entered for the world speed trials at Weymouth in 1972. But above all, Gerald Holtom will be remembered for his contribution to the nuclear disarmament movement that emerged in the 1950s in Britain. The biography focuses on this particular period and describes in detail how he designed the Peace Symbol and the visual display for the London to Aldermaston march.

In writing this biography I hope to have clarified the original significance of the Peace Symbol which, despite its worldwide use, remains somewhat obscure. I would also like to pay a tribute to my father and give him the recognition that he deserves for attempting to rid the world of nuclear weapons, as a first step towards world disarmament, through non-violent direct action.

A Safe Haven

Gerald Herbert Holtom was born in the seaside town of Sheringham in Norfolk, on 20 January 1914. It was an inauspicious time to be born, just six months before the outbreak of the First World War. Gerald's father, Edward Gibbs Holtom, was mobilised for military service, leaving behind him his wife Helen Quinton and their three sons, Philip, Bob and Gerald. It was thought that German troops might arrive from the North Sea and land on the Norfolk beaches, which were particularly vulnerable to invasion. The coast became strewn with barbed wire and gunfire crackled in the countryside, emanating from army training camps. When Zeppelins started drifting through the sky, Gerald's mother lost her nerve and decided to flee with her three sons to the relative safety of Worthing, on the south coast of England.

They were looked after by Helen's second cousin, Herbert Newton, who became Gerald's Godfather, and they lived together at the back of his shop on the seafront for the duration of the war. The shop sold a whole range of optical instruments including sextants, telescopes and microscopes. Gerald looked through a lens and was amazed to see the craters on the moon, or through another, protozoa oscillating their flagella in a drop of river water. Across the road the sea would heave and breathe, then crash onto the shore like a living being, imperceptibly stopping before drawing back a multitude of tiny streams to catch its breath again. The sea, the natural environment and, undeniably, the war would leave an everlasting impression on Gerald, influencing his works of art and his perception of the world.

At the end of the war, Helen returned with her three sons to Wiveton in Norfolk. They left Worthing by train and arrived at Liverpool Street Station in London, where Gerald, at the age of four, found himself perched on top of a huge pile of luggage, wearing his sailor's hat and clutching his teddy bear. The cast iron structure enveloping the station resembled an immense forest with metal trunks and branches stretching upwards to a smoked glass canopy. Horse drawn cabs were waiting outside. Motorcars with solid rubber tyres and spoked wheels darted about the streets alongside red buses with open tops; there were delivery vans of all descriptions and men wearing bowler hats. Children could be seen playing barefoot amongst errand boys on bicycles. Gerald looked around in bewilderment at the hordes of passengers who poured out of carriages onto the platform. A magnificent black and gold engine appeared, hissing steam and smelling of coal. This was their train for Norwich. The last stretch of the journey from Norwich to Holt was on a rustic set of passenger coaches with wooden seats that stopped at every village along the way. When they arrived in Holt, Helen and her three children gathered their belongings together and piled into an open taxi. The motorcar was equipped with a folding roof and elegant copper headlights which rumbled off over the dusty gravel roads in the direction of Wiveton.

The war was over, but would it be possible to reinstall a sense of continuity and security, or was life forever torn, shattered and changed beyond recognition? Helen was determined to find a safe haven for her family in the tranquility of the Norfolk villages and the beauty of the surrounding landscape. The taxi meandered through the Glaven Valley, passing water meadows and parks; some of the trees were strapped with wooden planks to protect them from cattle. They spotted a Georgian mansion proudly reflecting itself on the polished surface of a pond. There were hills covered in rhododendrons and pine trees with pale sandy trunks that lit up in the sunlight. Over the brow of a hill clusters of flintstone buildings with red tiled roofs appeared, then a medieval church and prominent landmarks such as the windmill at Cley and the lighthouse at Blakeney. The village of Wiveton was right next to the River Glaven which flowed down to the salt marshes and spilled into the North Sea. This was going to be their home for about a year and a half.

Gerald's father, Edward, survived the war but had been injured and shell-shocked and had to stay in hospital until the summer of 1919. He had been fortunate; many others had been disfigured or never came home, and those who did were disillusioned with heroism and probably wouldn't do anything they were told to do or taught to do again. Blakeney harbour had partially silted up and the carcass of a boat hull sat rotting in the mud. The grain barns were empty. However it was the unchanged landscape that healed the wounds and restored the soul. Houses, churches, clumps of trees and dykes were still the same. The migrating birds and the succession of the seasons continued. Rainbows appeared, thunderstorms groaned and lightning flickered across the slate grey sky as before. The lazy buzz of an

Gerald with his mother Helen, around 1917 ▶

insect in the dry summer grass could be heard again.

Gerald knew little about his father except that he was an architect, someone who could draw and design buildings, so when he came home he asked him to draw a train in a tunnel. Edward began to sketch the entrance of a tunnel that showed details of brickwork in the arch with small turrets on each side, and a hill behind with fields and trees. Railway lines and sleepers were added, then the entrance to the tunnel was filled with dark shading.

"Where is the train?" Gerald asked.

"It's in the tunnel, you can't see it", replied his father, who did know how to draw trains but probably needed a rest. As the days went by he produced drawings of all kinds of objects on request, including steam engines, and these drawing sessions were moments of great pleasure for both of them. He invented stories and took his sons for walks along the River Glaven. They sometimes spotted fish in the clear green water, betrayed by flashes of silver light from their bellies as they turned amongst the water weeds. Philip and Bob were excited about the prospects of fishing and Edward helped them make some rods out of bamboo. They used small pieces of bread for bait which they pressed around tiny barbed hooks. Gerald did not fish and preferred to watch the others, or the puffy white clouds change shape and their shadows that raced over the water meadow. Swallows glided low over the river then veered out of sight. Sunlight filtered through the translucent grass as it swayed in the breeze. He observed a glossy red ladybird struggling to climb the stem of a flower and a chalky yellow butterfly that danced beside him. Philip and Bob sat gripping their bamboo rods while Edward gazed at the coloured floats drifting slowly downstream. What had he seen in the trenches? The lines were reeled in and cast out again. A shadow loomed up close to one of the specks of bread, then with a flick of its tail it was gone.

The villages of Blakeney, Cley and Wiveton were collectively part of an important commercial port in the Middle Ages known as Blakeney Haven. Coal was later imported from Newcastle over the North Sea on brigs and coasters which returned with grain that was grown on the vast Holkham Estate. Trading with the use of large sailing vessels to Blakeney Harbour continued into the early 1900s. The tide then flowed over the mud flats and salt marshes through a labyrinth of channels and dykes. Gerald was immersed in this rural and coastal community that comprised a great variety of professions. There were farmers, fishermen and craftsmen of all kinds such as masons, carpenters, wheelwrights, sign writers and blacksmiths. The land was still worked by agricultural labourers in much the same way as it had been in the sixteenth century. There were scenes very similar to those portrayed by Breugel in his oil paintings such as *The Hay Harvest*, 1565.

The farm cottage where Gerald lived was largely self-sufficient. The farmers worked about sixty arduous hours a week and were hard put to earn a living, however they ate well and seemed to be happy. There was a latrine separated from the house that comprised a pear shaped hole in a scrubbed wooden bench. Drinking water was extracted from a well with a bucket and chain or from a squeaky hand pump. There were vegetable gardens, a workshop and a whole collection of farm animals including cows, horses and chickens. A large grinding wheel lapped up water from a trough when the iron handle was turned, which sharpened scythes and various other tools. Outbuildings housed wagons and ploughs, butter churns and dairy equipment.

Gerald was fascinated by the swallows and house martins that came in April to nest under the eaves of the house. He would watch them pick up pellets of mud from the edges of the duck pond to make nests, or follow their playful flight as they twisted and turned in the air and glided off in long straight lines. He was thrilled to see the young birds being fed and fly out from their little mud dwellings for the first time.

It was customary to celebrate the first of May with lilies of the valley which were offered as a symbol of hope, a new beginning and the change from winter to spring. Now that the war was over the celebration would have an even greater significance. Several people from the local community decided to organise a picnic outing to the woods at Holkham Hall, a few miles along the coast to the west of Wiveton. There was a great hustle and bustle early in the morning as the picnic was prepared. Everyone dressed in their finest clothes. Gerald was hoisted onto a horse driven wagon where people sat back to back on a bench running fore and aft. Hampers of food and crates of beer were loaded onto the wagon and various families joined along the way. The iron rims of the wheels crunched over the road and every time a steep hill was encountered the passengers would have to climb down and walk to the top. After much climbing on and off, the convoy eventually turned up a lane. There before them was Holkham Hall; a cream coloured palace on a huge field of grass that sloped away to distant sand hills and pine trees by the sea. They were greeted by the strident cry of a peacock and a magnificent display of iridescent feathers. Stags wandered nonchalantly over the parkland.

The lane rose gently into a cool dark wood full of very tall trees. Their trunks were devoid of branches up to a certain height. Shafts of light projected down onto clumps of bluebells from gaps in the canopy of leaves. They came to a scented part of the wood and sure enough, amongst the dingy undergrowth, the ground became speckled with a whole galaxy of white bell-shaped flowers. The horses were detached from their carts and the provisions were unloaded. Women laid blankets on the ground with crockery, glasses and almost everything you could imagine for the picnic lunch. There were all kinds of homemade pies and cakes, pickles, cold meat, cheese and fruit. The men took off their bowler hats and sipped their beer while the women and children scuttled into the woods with baskets to gather bunches of lilies of the valley.

Gerald's early life in Wiveton was intimately connected to the countryside around the Glaven estuary and the coast, where he could 'run wild' as his mother used to say. Sailing expeditions were organised to Blakeney Point at the end of a long sandy peninsula that curls out from the shore, renowned for its seal colonies and migrating birds. Many friends would meet up with sailing dinghies or fishing boats. On one occasion Gerald was taken aboard a sailing boat called the *Lead Kindly Light* and learnt the rudiments of sailing with one of the local fishermen. They left on the ebb of the tide at Morston and Gerald was shown how to sit on the weather side of the boat and operate the tiller. You had to look up at the corner of the sail where the gaff joined the mast and if it began to flap at that point you pulled the tiller towards you. As soon as the sail was full you straightened the tiller to keep the sail correctly set to the wind. When the boats were beached at Blakeney Point the children scrambled out to explore the sandhills, paddle in the sea and gather cockles.

Destined to become an Artist

The Holtom family moved from Wiveton in 1920 and went to live in the market town of Holt, a few miles to the east and further inland from the sea. Gerald's domestic environment was now reduced to a narrow lawn at the back of Yew Tree Cottage where he played with lead soldiers by himself or croquet with his brothers. He enjoyed watching the beekeeper next door, dressed in a straw hat and a veil, puff smoke into a hive with small bellows. Edward fixed a brass plate on the garden gate with the inscriptions E.G. Holtom FRIBA Architect and Surveyor.

Gerald would no longer be running wild over the salt marshes and at the age of six he went to a Dame School at the other end of town called The Limes. This was a private nursery run by a woman from her own home, where he learnt the rudiments of mathematics and how to read and write. On his way to school he would pass by a tobacconist's, a haberdasher's and numerous pubs and sweet shops. There were people mounting bicycles from a little wooden step on the hub of the back wheel. Sometimes he would be startled by the squeal of a pig being slaughtered at the market. Once a day at The Limes the children were released onto the Spout Hills, where they fought mock battles and hid behind blackberry bushes or climbed trees. Newcomers would have to prove their worth or remain outcasts. Gerald saw much less of his brothers who went to the junior school at Gresham's, known as the Old School House, and almost everything he did was now supervised.

Edward's architectural practice began to flourish. He joined partnership with John Page, who was another architect from Blakeney, and they worked from their office in Fakenham. With new prospects and Helen's desire to run a school as she had once done before the war, Edward decided to move the family to a more spacious place in Station Road, called The Acacias, which overlooked the playing fields of the Old School House. There was a wild garden that had been neglected for many years and had become overgrown with brambles. This was soon cleared to reveal some old acacia trees, numerous fruit trees, decorative shrubs and a lawn.

There was also a greenhouse and a potting shed for growing vegetables. The building itself had Victorian gables, bay windows and a square porch. Helen wanted to use The Acacias as a residential school for young children and this venture proved to be a success.

Gerald was enchanted by the magical garden and the numerous visitors who called by. His bedroom was in a small room above the porch which had several large windows that gave him views of the Old School House and playing fields beyond the wall across the road. He liked to watch the sky change colour early in the morning and the chaotic flight of rooks as they attempted to land in the gusty wind. There were two cavities left in the garden wall from missing stones which were used as footholds by Bob and Philip who used to climb over the wall to school.

The Acacias overlooked an immaculate bowling green. During the long summer evenings Gerald would secretly climb onto the potting shed with his friends and hide amongst the ivy to watch the gentlemen of Holt play bowls. The children grabbed apples from the overhanging trees and munched them in silence, trying not to laugh at the comical spectacle. Each bowler had his own particular stride and made all kinds of gesticulations in an attempt to steer a wayward wood towards the jack. Some ran on tiptoes leaning over sideways while others flapped their arms in desperation. Gerald imagined drawing these scenes. He had been impressed by some figurative drawings made by his brother's friends and was shown engravings of caricatures made by the French artist Honoré Daumier.

Gerald's parents encouraged him to draw and paint from an early age. Edward showed him perspective tricks, horizons and vanishing points as well as how to put a wash of watercolour onto a tilted sketch book without leaving streaks. Helen knew two local artists. One of them was Lawrence Linnell who earned a living entirely from painting watercolours and making pastel drawings of local scenes. The other artist was Gerald Ackermann who was also a landscape painter and often visited Blakeney. He was an artist whom Helen had always admired, so much so that she named her son after him.

Gerald made sketches of the garden at The Acacias and a painting of the wisteria that climbed around the bay windows and up to the eves of the house. One of his first small drawings of Blakeney Point that he made when he was six was framed and hung on the wall in his parents' bedroom. On one fateful day he was given a paint box full of watercolours and told that he was going to be an artist. From then on he made a habit of going out to places on his bicycle, with a haversack carefully loaded

An early watercolour painting of gorse on the Norfolk landscape by Gerald

An early watercolour painting of the Norfolk coast by Gerald

with brushes, paper, water and his precious box of paints.

Lawrence Linnell began to show an interest in Gerald's early paintings and found them promising. He offered to be his art tutor and invited him to go out painting in the Norfolk landscapes. They cycled out to a site at a particular time of day when the light would be right and set up their easels to paint for two or three hours without a pause. Linnell liked to paint early sunrises and late sunsets, blackthorn in the hedgerows, rhododendrons, azaleas and pine trees. He painted gorse on the heathland, cornfields, poppies, wild apple blossom and sea lavender. They would go out to paint the salt marshes and the mudflats or the sand hills and the sea. People or buildings were rarely portrayed.

Painting the Norfolk landscapes alternated with a variety of outdoor sports. During the summer months Gerald went swimming in the sea with his brothers and friends at Sheringham and sailed at Blakeney. In the winter they went tobogganing on the Spout Hills or skated on frozen ponds.

Inevitably the time came when Gerald was measured up and fitted out with a blazer, long grey trousers and a white shirt. The blazer had flat brass buttons and a coloured shield. After slackening his tie, he swivelled on his school cap and climbed over the garden wall to Gresham's school for boys. It was compulsory for the school children to attend Chapel on Sundays; cycling was forbidden on a Sunday unless you were given special permission from the headmaster. Hands in pockets were not allowed at school and many of the pockets were sewn up for this reason. They would assemble in lines in front of the Chapel, all smartly dressed in their straw hats, then file into rows of pews to the left and right of the main aisle. The lectern, made of oak and carved into an eagle, perched motionless on the cold stone floor in front of the altar. One of the drawbacks of the architectural layout, with the pews facing parallel to the aisle, was that you had to twist your head sideways to look at the speaker. Gerald found this so uncomfortable that he had no recollection whatsoever of anything preached in a sermon.

Then came the Officers' Training Corps, where the boys marched and counter marched on the school parade ground carrying Enfield rifles. They were taught techniques of infantry warfare on Kelling Heath and attended army camps in Aldershot. There was a military band with drums and bugles led by an officer twiddling a white stick. All uniforms were immaculate and boots and belts were highly polished. On one of these occasions Gerald found himself marching alongside Benjamin Britten who, with his enigmatic smile, deliberately stepped out of time, much to the annoyance of the sergeant major.

Outings were organised by some of the staff to go target shooting on the deserted heather ranges. At the impressionable age of fourteen, Gerald found himself in an open Crossley Charabanc loaded with guns, telescopic sights and live ammunition. Novices began as 'spotters' and were placed in a trench directly below a row of targets. Their job was to indicate the score to the shooters who shot from 200 and 500 yards away. Bullets ripped through the paper targets above their heads and thudded into the sandbank behind. The targets were mounted on a hinged frame that could be cranked down to the horizontal and the 'spotters' stuck small black squares of paper over each bullet hole. They raised the frame and then held up a disc on the end of a long stick which was waved about in a coded manner to indicate the score. The outings were informal and convivial with a picnic at lunchtime and afternoon tea. They were taught the safety procedures for handling guns and how to adjust their aims for the prevailing wind conditions. Ironically, Gerald's sharp eye and steady grip that enabled him to paint the Norfolk landscapes were also used to pull the trigger of a gun.

Gerald liked the art classes best, where you could paint, do anything or nothing. He became Miss Bristow's favorite and was delighted but somewhat perplexed to receive the art prize at the end of the year. She was a very dedicated and enthusiastic art teacher, who organised outings with her pupils to draw and paint in the surrounding countryside. She used to hire an open taxi for herself and the youngest boys while the older ones rode on their bicycles. They loaded up with picnics and all the necessary art equipment, then headed off to the salt marshes and woods full of bluebells, or to the sandy beaches along the coast. Sometimes they would stop and look at a cluster of majestic pine trees or explore the water meadows in search of a good composition. The children toiled away with their paint brushes, trying to express what they saw, gradually developing their own particular style, and above all learnt how to observe. There were no rules, you could draw whatever you imagined. Peter Floud's sketchbook overflowed with coils of exotic dragons.

When Armistice Day came on 11 November, all classwork was put aside and the teachers would describe events of the war from their own experiences. The children listened in silence and tried to imagine what it must have been like to scramble out of a rat infested trench into barbed wire and machine gun fire, like one of the soldiers in Paul Nash's oil painting *Over the Top*, 1918. Music recitals took place at the school on

Saturday evenings and at the back of the hall there was a balcony full of library books including volumes of *The Times History of the War*. These volumes were illustrated with numerous photographs that Gerald and his friends, including Benjamin Britten, used to browse through as they listened to the music.

Benjamin Britten was a pacifist and later became a well-known musical composer. His *War Requiem* would later become one of Gerald's favorite musical compositions. On the book shelves they began to learn about the more obscure facts of the war and were stunned to discover the football matches that took place on No Man's Land. It became apparent that the war had been contrived by a handful of men and fought by millions, driven by patriotic heroism, to rot on the battlefields. The hypocrisy of the war and the shocking truth was also revealed by Henri Barbusse in his book *Under Fire*, 1916, written from his own experiences in the trenches of Northern France.

Towards the end of his time at Gresham's, Gerald suffered a knee injury caused by the combined effects of playing rugby and intensive training for the long jump. All sports had to be postponed and he went to convalesce with his aunts, Alice and Hettie, who lived in Stratford Upon Avon. It was an occasion for Gerald to focus on his painting and also to share his aunts' passion for the theatre. They lived in a Tudor house made from black oak timbers and wattle and daub that had been renovated by Edward. The windows had original Elizabethan glass set in lead lozenges and the floor was made of broad oak planks that had been roughly trimmed with an adze. Gerald was taken to see a number of Shakespeare plays that were performed on a small cinema stage in the town and these would be enthusiastically discussed and commented on afterwards. Gerald began to sell a few of his watercolour paintings and thought about travelling to some of the remoter parts of Norfolk to paint. His aunts suggested going on a motorbike if he was unable to cycle. A deal was made. With Gerald's savings and a generous contribution on their behalf, he later returned to Holt with a 250cc *Excelsior*...and a note for his mother that read *'for sketching purposes only.'*

It was becoming clear that Gerald was going to be an artist. He hadn't been pleased with his academic achievements and had, as he said, a real fear of his abundant inabilities. However his passion for sport and art had given him confidence. Gerald noted: '*I was rather backward, good at sport and happiest when painting watercolours by myself.*'

Watercolour painting of Norwich by Gerald, 1931

Art School

Gerald was devoted to painting and had his mind set on going to art school. Several artists he knew suggested applying to the Royal College of Art. A letter was sent to the principal of the RCA, Sir William Rothenstein, enclosing recommendations from the headmaster at Gresham's and the painter Ackermann. Rothenstein advised Gerald to go to the Norwich School of Art for a year first, then sit the RCA entrance exam in London.

Gerald was accepted at the Norwich School of Art in 1931. This coincided with an economic slump that swept across Britain; Edward's architectural practice diminished and Helen's school became depleted. Philip needed money to study at Cambridge University and the mortgage still had to be paid on The Acacias. Bob, who had just got a job at a bank in Worthing, was the only member of the family to have a regular wage.

Unaware of the growing crisis, Gerald set off over the gritty roads to Norwich on his *Excelsior*. He stayed at a boarding house on the Newmarket Road during the week and returned home for the weekends. Norwich School of Art had been established in 1845 and the building itself was made of red brick with a lively set of windows that overlooked the river Wensum. The bricks were glazed to a certain height in the corridors and the rooms were crammed with plaster casts of antique heads and figures.

They were a small group of students with ages ranging from fourteen to seventy. Sketches were made of the antique replicas and they attended life drawing classes where they tried to fathom the anatomy of fully clothed models. Their friendly art teacher Horace Tuck, who specialised in watercolour and oil painting, emphasized the importance of perspective in their work. One student drew everything he saw, filling sketch books with smeared ink, pencil and chalk. Another student, a beautiful girl from the 'top drawer' of society, came to paint flowers with her mother. She could have been just the right person to fall in love with, but remained destined for dreams. Gerald contented himself with heavy lined portraits of his fellow students, and looked forward to joining the Norwich Rugby Club where he was going to train hard and play on the left wing.

Norwich was a wonderful place to study for any art student. Gerald used to go to the Castle Museum to look at watercolour paintings made by John Sell Cotman. Many of these were protected by a velvet curtain to prevent the colours from fading. It was magical to draw back the curtains and discover landscapes full of ploughed fields and rivers, or yellow mustard flowers in full bloom. Norwich Cathedral was another inspiration with its impressive stone columns and ogives that splayed into carved ceiling bosses. In other parts of the city, Tudor houses built from heavy oak frames leant over cobbled streets and clung to flintstone walls.

After an intensive and successful year in Norwich, Gerald was looking forward to the summer vacation when he would see his family, meet up with old friends, and perhaps have a few rounds of tennis or go swimming in the sea. However, these fine prospects were marred by financial difficulties at home. Edward was on the verge of bankruptcy and the mortgage could not be paid. Fortunately for Gerald, the studentship for his next year at art school could be covered by funds from Gresham's, investment from Bob, and contributions from Hettie and Alice. In September 1932, Gerald packed some cases with sketch books, a handmade pallet for oil painting and a folded easel, not forgetting his rugby kit. These were firmly strapped to the *Excelsior* and after a few sorrowful goodbyes from his parents, Gerald set off to London. The Royal College of Art was tucked behind the Victoria and Albert Museum on Exhibition Road and the entrance exam was going to take place on a Monday morning. The studio had faded cream coloured walls, embellished with green paint, and a cast iron spiral staircase in one corner. There were about thirty candidates and the examination involved drawing a nude Italian model. Some of the students stood at easels while others sat astride 'donkeys,' which were benches that had angled supports for a drawing board at one end. Gerald had never used paper the size of a poster before or drawn for so long. The students went to relax in the common room during the lunch break where they sat in battered chairs around trestle tables and talked amongst themselves. There was a small stage at the back of the room and a gymnasium behind. Was this going to be their home for the next

Life drawing by Gerald, 1933 ▶

Oct 20"/33.

three years? Life drawing continued in the afternoon and at the end of the examination the students waited nervously in the corridor for their results. Gerald was the last to be ushered into the office where the registrar, looking as sad as a Saint Bernard, announced:

"I'm sorry to say you have failed."

After his initial disappointment, and after making a number of inquiries, Gerald was offered a place at the Hornsey School of Art where he joined a small group of friendly students in a well-lit studio. They were busy life drawing or 'drawing from the nude' as it was sometimes called. There before them was a beautiful naked young woman propped up on a high stool. Gerald felt like an intruder at first, but she seemed perfectly content to be sitting there and to be admired hour after hour with her long dark hair flowing down over her slender arms. The art teacher was enthusiastic and gave demonstrations of how to create form, space and structure, advising them to always look at something as if it was for the first time, which in this case for Gerald it certainly was.

Gerald attended these life drawing sessions for the next fortnight. However, despite the favourable conditions and the good atmosphere, he still had his heart set on going to the RCA. He decided to contact Rothenstein to ask him if he could show him more of his drawings, and perhaps be given a second chance. Rothenstein agreed to meet him with his work. Against all odds, and after a long, agonising pause, he turned to Gerald and said "You shall come to the College".

Gerald was overjoyed and moved into a room on the first floor of a house in Powis Terrace. On some occasions a piano could be heard trundling along the road below. The sound would become louder, then stop. After a short pause the neighbourhood would spring to life with Strauss waltzes that filtered through the streets. When the music ended, sash windows went up with cheers of applause and people threw out coins for the pianist, wrapped in little paper packets to prevent them rolling away on the pavement.

On his way to the RCA in the morning, Gerald walked through Kensington Gardens and along a wide avenue of giant elms. Sometimes he strolled past the Serpentine Lake in Hyde Park or stopped at the Round Pond where retired admirals and children sailed their model yachts and ocean liners. The spires of Whitechapel could be glimpsed at times in the distance.

One of his first assignments involved making architectural

drawings of historical shop fronts that were on display at the Victoria and Albert Museum. Gerald measured up an 18th century bow window with the help of his fellow students, then drew it to scale in the architectural studio. Much of the time in the first year was dedicated to life drawing. They were expected to 'draw from the nude' on at least three days a week and there was also an evening session open to students as well as members of the public. These evening sessions were often crammed full. A thicket of mature students stood at the back of the room working from easels, while others perched themselves on chairs holding their drawing boards or worked close up on 'donkeys'. It was on one of these occasions that Gerald's attention was drawn to Madeleine Anderson who had found space to draw from a step halfway up the spiral staircase. Madeleine had already painted for three years at The Kingston-Upon-Thames School of Art and most of the students had been to art schools for several years before coming to the RCA. Gerald was in at the deep end. Some teachers gave encouragement, others pulled you to pieces without mercy. Charles Mahoney was one of the painting teachers who gathered up their drawing boards at the end of each session and commented on their work. Barnett Freedman and Gilbert Spencer were art teachers who were particularly enthusiastic and their explanations of colour relationships and demonstrations with paint mixing were inspirational.

Lunchtime in the common room was a welcome break after drawing all morning. It was also a time to meet fellow students and discuss important world affairs, particularly the Disarmament Conferences that took place between 1932 and 1934. They talked about pacifism and how future conflicts might be avoided through international cooperation.

Many students at the RCA lived on the poverty line and only a minority came from middle class or 'top drawer' backgrounds. They often went hungry, wore tatty clothes and walked long distances to save bus fares. However, the museums and galleries were free. Regular visits were made to the National Gallery, the Tate and a whole collection of small exhibitions around Bond Street where they could immerse themselves in surrealism or impressionism. Students at the RCA were given free access to the libraries in the Victoria and Albert Museum and the British Museum.

As well as enjoying the multitude of cultural possibilities that London had to offer, Gerald was keen to pursue his rugby. He joined the RCA Rugby Club which not only widened his circle of friends but also led to an unexpected outcome. The players were a rough and enthusiastic crew who played against the Metropolitan Police, the Scots Guards and several other London Universities on suburban playing fields. After the matches the team's successes and failures were announced during the lunch hour in the common room, which would be accompanied with cheers or boos as appropriate. These matches began to arouse curiosity among some of the women students who went out in all weathers to support them. By the end of his second year Gerald had become captain of the RCA rugby team and recalls playing full back in a match against a battalion of heavily built Scots Guards in Twickenham. As he ran for the line he was grabbed by the ankles by one and tackled high by another, crashing head first onto the ground. He then remembers waking up in Putney Hospital on a trolley with a terrible headache and black eyes. Madeleine had accompanied him in the ambulance from the playing field and, after Gerald had been diagnosed with concussion, she took him home to rest, with the instructions 'not to be left alone'.

Gerald and Madeleine moved into a flat on Redcliffe Road with their friend John Burrell, for their third and final year at the RCA. There were two rooms and a kitchen with a bath under a hinged lid that served as the kitchen table. Coal was delivered by horse and cart and muffins were sold in the street. John had studied sculpture and painting but his main interest was the theatre. He spent most of his time producing plays on the little common room stage at the RCA with some of the students, including Gerald. He later became co-director of the Old Vic Theatre and a founder of the American Shakespeare Festival Theatre in Connecticut.

John had a gramophone that he called the 'groan', and a vast collection of classical music and jazz records that were played at various times of day to suit particular moods. He had a flair for discovering all kinds of special events in London and took Madeleine and Gerald to the Alhambra music hall in Leicester Square to see the Ballet Russe de Monte Carlo. John drove home to Shropshire at the weekends and on one occasion offered to drop Gerald and Madeleine off in the Cotswolds on his way, so that they could paint together, and pick them up on his way back on Sunday afternoon. This they happily agreed to and the three of them set off early one cloudless Saturday morning in his tiny MG motorcar. John drove them to a field of luminous yellow mustard flowers where they unloaded the easels and a tent, then said their goodbyes. Soon the little car was just a speck on the horizon. Looking around they saw an old farmhouse and dry-stone walls that contoured the hills and surrounding fields. Gerald and Madeleine painted all day and pinned up their canvases to dry, overwhelmed by the heavy scent and smoke from the campfire.

The next day a luxuriant myriad of wildflowers glistened in the morning dew and skylarks sang above the meadows. They continued to paint until they heard hoots from the road and soon they were off at breakneck speed to Redcliffe Road, drowsy and sunburnt.

A Conscientious Objector

Gerald finished his studies at the Royal College of Art in 1935. It was the same year that Britain signed the Anglo-German Naval Agreement. All the London Naval Conferences that took place between December 1935 and March 1936, for the purpose of limiting the manufacture of warships and submarines among world powers, ended in failure. The future was looking ominous.

Gerald and Madeleine became married and lived in Willow Road, London. They began to earn a living as artists by exhibiting their work at various London galleries and selling their paintings. Their first child, Peter, was born in 1936. Gerald found employment as an art teacher at a grammar school in Hertfordshire for a year and then left teaching to specialise in cotton printing. He made designs for furniture fabric that were inspired by traditional African and Indian wood block prints and Australian Aboriginal art. His designs were full of floral and geometrical shapes with spirals and abstract forms as well as elephants, birds, lizards and fish. He was influenced by the work of the textile designer William Morris (1834-1896). Gerald established a furniture shop in Tottenham Court Road in 1937 where he sold his own printed textiles together with work made by other artists and craftsmen, including rugs and handmade wooden chairs. One day, completely by chance, Peter Floud, who had attended Miss Bristow's sketching outings with Gerald at Gresham's, went into his shop and discovered his work. He liked the designs and took away samples to exhibit at the Victoria and Albert Museum where he worked.

In September 1938, Gerald took a short break from the city and went to immerse himself in the natural surroundings of Stiffkey Creek in Norfolk, preoccupied by the possibility of another war. It was a wild place. As he walked over the dykes, deep in thought, a cormorant popped its head out from a narrow channel. The tide came in and flooded the sand. There was a strong clear wind and ripples came in hundreds of thousands, lapping and hissing across the bay. The brown sand darkened and became pitted, as rough as a flintstone wall, with each little mound casting its shadow.

The Second World War was declared a year later, in September 1939. It was also the year that Madeleine gave birth to their second child, Julia. The furniture shop was requisitioned by the council for use as an air raid shelter and Gerald left London to do agricultural work in Suffolk, provisionally registered as a conscientious objector. He wrote: *'A cause of war appears to me to be that, where creative activity is stifled and profit is the absorbing primary consideration, men are willing to turn to the intriguing machines of destruction.'* As a pacifist, Gerald stated: *'A man can use no armaments to defend his ideals of human life if his highest ideal is to lay down his life and if destruction is the most debased action.'*

At the beginning of the war Gerald was employed as a market gardener on Assington Hall Farm, where they grew all kinds of vegetables. One of his jobs was to shovel lime onto the land from a wheelbarrow. In the colder months the lime scattered across patches of ice that reflected the blue sky above. Gerald wrote: *'by the end of the year the whole of the Constable country was shedding its leaves, ambitious ideas, hopes and fruit of a year's work, to decompose and lie dormant through the winter.'*

Unknown to Gerald, an ominous discovery was being made in another part of the country. Otto Frisch and Rudolf Peierls, two scientists working at the University of Birmingham, had just resolved the peculiar problem of determining the critical mass of uranium 235. In March 1940 they produced the first technical exposition of how to make an atomic bomb that could be dropped from a plane. In the Frisch-Peierls Memorandum they described how the energy stored in the atomic nuclei could be liberated: *'This energy is liberated in a small volume, in which it will, for an instant, produce a temperature comparable to that in the interior of the sun. The blast from such an explosion would destroy life in a wide area. The size of this area is difficult to estimate, but it will probably cover the centre of a big city. In addition, some part of the energy set free by the bomb goes to produce radioactive substances, and these will emit very powerful and dangerous radiation.'* This information led to a flurry of research at some of Britain's most reputable universities, resulting in the British and Canadian research and development programme for nuclear weapons, code-named 'Tube Alloys'.

Gerald recalls looking out of the window of his room in Assington and seeing a magnificent beech tree and a giant holly. *'The sky had become entirely grey, like a balloon or dome enclosing the little room. Any attempts at penetrating beyond seemed hopeless and rather frightening.'* Gerald's application to be registered as a conscientious objector turned out to be unfavourable and he was taken to Chelmsford Prison in November 1942. First offenders were put into huts where the clamour was so intense that one's mind had to struggle to preserve its own identity. Gerald was pleased to discover a plot of land where they could do gardening. There were even some ash trees and roses. In December 1942 he was transferred to Wormwood Scrubs Prison. *'Footsteps came, a thumb pushed a switch and the heavy walls dissolved into darkness.'*

Madeleine sent a letter to an appeal tribunal in support of Gerald's pacifism. He was later released from prison and commanded to do agricultural work in Suffolk for the rest of the war. Gerald was joined by his family at Grove Farm in Edwardstone where their third child, Anna, was born in 1943. Work on the farm involved threshing barley and oats, chopping out sugar beet and carting wheat. An enormous straw stack was built beside the farmhouse that provided shelter from the strong wind.

On the other side of the Atlantic, Tube Alloys had been collaborating with the Manhattan Project in the USA to produce the most atrocious device ever conceived by man: the atomic bomb. Vast stocks of uranium had been shipped to New York from the Shinkolobwe mine in the Congo.

6 August 1945

A Japanese history professor recalls what he saw from Hijiyama Hill:

"I saw that Hiroshima had disappeared. I was shocked by the sight. What I felt then and feel now I just can't explain with words. Of course I saw many dreadful scenes after that, but that experience, looking down and finding nothing left of Hiroshima was so shocking that I simply can't express what I felt."

The atomic bombings of the two Japanese cities, Hiroshima on 6 August 1945, and Nagasaki three days later, were the most devastating attacks in military history. Living organisms instantly perished. Flowers, trees, grass, plants all shrivelled up and died. The air itself was burnt away. Metal vaporised and rocks melted. Men, women and children perished instantly or suffered terrible burns and became blind. Many died later from radiation sickness or from cancer caused by the radioactive emissions in the years to come.

This tragedy marked the beginning of a new era where the word 'peace' came to mean little more than a balance of terror. The writer and activist Arthur Koestler wrote shortly afterwards:

'If I were asked to name the most important date in the history of the human race, I would answer without hesitation the 6th of August 1945. From the dawn of consciousness until the 6th of August 1945, man had to live with the prospect of his death as an individual; since the day when the first atomic bomb out-shone the sun over Hiroshima, he has had to live with the prospect of his extinction as a species.'

[*Sanity*, CND periodical, August 1983]

Waking up to Evil

While technological advances have followed an exponential curve, ethical and environmental progress appear to have lagged behind. In the words of the peace advocate Norman Cousins, *"Man has exalted change in everything but himself. He has leaped centuries ahead in inventing a new world to live in, but he knows little or nothing about his own part in that world".*

The atomic bombings of Hiroshima and Nagasaki profoundly shocked the world population. In spite of this, scientific research institutions for nuclear weapons proliferated. By the end of the 1950s, Britain, Russia and the United States of America had set up atomic test sites across the globe from Australia to Kazakhstan. This resulted in widespread radioactive pollution and a new range of thermonuclear weapons a *thousand* times more deadly than those dropped on the Japanese cities, such as the US hydrogen bomb detonated over Bikini Atoll in 1954.

With the scientific expertise of William Penny and his team from the newly formed UK Atomic Weapons Research Establishment (AWRE) in Aldermaston, the British government pursued a devastating series of atomic bomb tests. These occurred in the Montebello islands, Australia, Malden Island and Christmas Island in the Pacific Ocean, from 1952 to 1958. Major test explosions were announced in the public media but the general public had little specific knowledge about the nuclear testing programme as this was kept under a shroud of secrecy. Public awareness and opposition were also slow to develop due to the remoteness of the sites.

Britain's first nuclear bomb test took place in a lagoon next to Trimouille Island in the Montebello archipelago, off the north-west coast of Australia, on 3 October 1952. This plutonium device ripped a massive hole in the seabed and caused widespread ecological damage. The mushroom cloud spread radioactive fallout across large portions of Australia, contaminating the air, food and water. The presence of Aboriginal populations on the mainland near to the Montebello Islands and their vulnerability to the fallout had been totally disregarded by the AWRE.

On 15 October 1953, Yami Lester, a ten year old Aboriginal boy, was staying with his family at Wallantinna station. Early in the morning he remembers being startled by a rumbling sound coming from the south:

"I looked up south and saw this black smoke rolling through the mulga. It just came at us through the trees like a big, black mist. The old people started shouting 'it's a mamu' (evil spirit). They dug holes in the sand dune and told us to get in. We got in and it rolled over and around us and went away. Everyone was vomiting and had diarrhoea and people were laid out everywhere. The next day people had very sore eyes, red with tears, and I could not open my eyes. Five days after the black cloud came, the old people started dying".

[*The Observer*, 3 April 1983]

The black mist was in fact the dust cloud, full of radioactive plutonium, from the British nuclear test at Emu Field. Yami Lester survived but lost his sight as a result.

The British authorities set up another site to the south of Emu Field at Maralinga, where various atomic tests took place between 1956 and 1957. Aboriginal populations were forced to leave the area and were sent to camps at Yalata on the south coast of the Nullarbor Plain. This led to social disintegration, loss of identity and alcoholism.

A traditional Aboriginal route crossed through the nuclear test site at Maralinga. The Tjarutja population, unaware of the dangers, wandered barefoot over contaminated ground and families were even found camping in the craters made by the atomic tests. No health records were kept on the Aboriginal population. Secret Aldermaston documents showed later that the ground was highly radioactive around Maralinga, contaminated by uranium, beryllium and plutonium, one of the most toxic radionuclides with a half-life of 24,000 years. It took another ten years, after the nuclear tests had finished, before some of the radioactive debris was superficially ploughed into the ground.

Yami Lester became a key figure in the anti-nuclear movement in South Australia and his devoted campaigning led to the McClelland Royal Commission Inquiry (1984-1985). It wasn't until 2000 that Maralinga and Emu Field were officially decontaminated by the Australian government, at a cost of over a hundred million Australian dollars. In 2021 research carried out at the Monash University in Australia revealed that radioactive particles still persist in the soil. The natural process of erosion could bring about the slow release of plutonium in the years to come, which would be absorbed by wildlife.

After testing atomic weapons on Australian territory, the British nuclear team then moved to the Line Islands in the central Pacific Ocean, which used to be part of the British Gilbert and Ellice Islands Colony. They undertook a number of atmospheric nuclear explosions over Malden Island and Christmas Island between 1957 and 1958. Their particular objective was to test a thermonuclear bomb, otherwise known as the hydrogen bomb or H-bomb. Over fourteen thousand British personnel and scientific staff were sent out for this purpose.

The decision to construct the hydrogen bomb, on 16 June 1954, had taken place in secrecy at a meeting with Sir Winston Churchill and the Defence Committee of the British Cabinet. It was not until 7 June 1956 that Sir Anthony Eden, Churchill's successor, made a statement to the House of Commons confirming that a thermonuclear weapon would be tested in a remote place in the Pacific Ocean.

On 17 October 1956 the world's first nuclear reactor was inaugurated in Britain at the Windscale site on the north-west coast of England. Its *primary* use was for producing plutonium for the manufacture of atomic weapons at the AWRE in Aldermaston and in the USA. Electricity production was a secondary function. Nuclear power and nuclear weapons became intrinsically linked and produced highly toxic radioactive waste. This marked the beginning of an industry that would become responsible for the world's worst ever environmental and public health concerns that humanity has had to deal with, and would continue to do so for a little less than eternity. On 10 October 1957, just one year after starting, there was a serious nuclear accident at the Windscale plant that led to widespread radioactive contamination and an increase in cancer in the local community.

Various individuals, including Gerald, were beginning to wake up to Britain's H-bomb test, planned for 1957 in Polynesia. Harold Steele was an English pacifist from Great Malvern who believed in direct nonviolent action as a means to oppose war and violence. He had been a conscientious objector during the First World War and was a member of the No Conscription Fellowship. Because of his pacifist views he had been sentenced to seven years hard labour and had to spend three years in prison. He was determined to put an end to the nuclear testing and planned to sail from Japan with his wife to the blast zone of the British H-bomb test in the central Pacific. Harold Steele told reporters:

"My wife and I are prepared to end our days in pain to prove how horrible the effects of nuclear radiation can be. The time has come for

someone to make a real move to stop the tests ... I believe this demonstration will shake the conscience of man out of its lazy acceptance of the H-bomb and all its horrors". [Grappling with the Bomb: Britain's Pacific H-bomb Tests, Nic Maclellan, 2017]

The Emergency Committee for Direct Action Against Nuclear War was set up in London to raise funds for Harold Steele's mission, together with support from the Peace Pledge Union and the philosopher Bertrand Russell. Steele went alone via India but was unable to reach Japan before the first H-bomb exploded over Malden Island on 15 May 1957. The test caused international outrage. An estimated 350,000 people protested across Japan. 20,000 students demonstrated around the British Embassy and 3000 school children held a lantern procession. Steele arrived in Japan two days after the first explosion and endeavoured to organise a crew to sail to Christmas Island with the hope of stopping further H-bomb testing. He was unable to get the necessary backing and returned to England in June 1957 to focus on changing public opinion. He laid down the foundations for nuclear protest in the UK, with the formation of the Direct Action Committee Against Nuclear War (DAC).

On 8 November 1957, a Hydrogen bomb was detonated over Christmas Island, followed by another on 28 April 1958. The British government downplayed concerns about radioactive fallout from the tests and gave little consideration to the local Gilbertese population. As well as the DAC, another nuclear protest organisation emerged. This was the Campaign for Nuclear Disarmament (CND). The philosopher Bertrand Russell was their president, with Canon John Collins their chairman and Peggy Duff their secretary. The inaugural meeting of CND took place in London on 17 February 1958 at Central Hall, Westminster. Speakers included Russell, the historian Alan Taylor, the writer John Priestley, the politician Michael Foot and the naval officer Stephen King-Hall.

Gerald had been told about this public meeting and set off early with his wife and children, so they could have seats near the front. The main hall itself, as well as a number of overflow halls, all filled up to their maximum capacity with about 5000 people, which was phenomenal. The audience was a typical cross section of society; there were teachers, parents with children, teenagers and a sprinkling of older people. Russell gave the following speech:

"The world at present is rushing towards disaster. At present it seems an even chance whether any human beings exist forty years hence. If man

is to survive, the trend must be reversed. A number of measures will be necessary, some fairly easy, others very difficult. I will take the easiest measures first.

Nuclear tests must be stopped

The harm that is being done by tests is not generally realised, especially as it is cumulative. Sea and rain, in most parts of the world, have become radio-active in varying degrees. Unfortunately, animals and plants concentrate the radio-active material and become much more affected than the water and soil upon which they depend. The US Navy, in the neighbourhood of Bikini, found that some clams which they had examined were 2000 times as radio-active as the water in which they lived. Radioactive Strontium 90, an artificial substance resulting from nuclear tests, is now found in all parts of the world. It accumulates in bones especially and causes cancer as well as mutations of genes. The British Atomic Scientists' Association has calculated that the Bikini tests probably caused some 50,000 cancers. How many mental defects they will cause it is as yet impossible to guess. If you give one man cancer or cause one child to be born an idiot, you are a monster; but if you do the same injury to 50,000 you are a patriot. It is odd that the same governments which promote expensive research to combat cancer, also employ still more expensive methods of increasing it. Although Great Britain is far removed from all the places where tests have taken place, Strontium 90, in continually increasing quantities, has been found in this country in grass and milk. Each test increases this amount. The tests, if continued, will kill all fish, make meat and milk poisonous, and cause genetic damage which will continue through thousands of years if the race survives. If agreement to stop the tests should not prove possible, Great Britain alone should abandon tests. It is intolerable that our country should be an accomplice in this vast atrocity.

The danger of a great war by accident must be minimised

As we have lately learnt, planes carrying H-bombs are continually flying over Great Britain. The Prime Minister has assured us that this involves no new danger since, if the planes crash, the bombs will not explode. This, though perhaps literally true, is a misleading statement. New Scientist, on January 2nd, pointed out that the bombs carry plutonium which, even in the absence of a full explosion, would cause very grave damage. It is a highly poisonous substance of which 0.6 millionth of a gram is considered the largest permissible dose. As its half-life is 24,000 years, its escape would mean that a large area would have to be evacuated for a long time, and all cattle and vegetables in the area would have to be destroyed. This, however, is not the gravest danger due to planes carrying H-bombs. A much graver danger is that of accidents mistakenly attributed to enemy action, which might easily precipitate a great war that no one has intended. This is more likely since it is generally assumed that a war would begin with the destruction of capital cities and would have to be carried out without orders from the central government. Such great military advantages attach to a surprise attack that each side expects the enemy to resort to it. This inevitably produces a state of nerves of which the disastrous consequences are immeasurable. Great Britain ought, not only for the good of the world, but even on the narrowest grounds of national interests, to refuse missile bases on its territory. The Defence Minister stated that frankly, in the event of war, the government could not protect the population, but only missile stations and aeroplane bases. Since it is these that would cause the motive for attack, it is clear that we are safer without them.

The spread of H-bombs must be stopped

Caligula wished that he could exterminate all his enemies with one blow. He was thought to be mad. There are now three Caligulas in the world; Great Britain, the US and USSR, who actually possess the power that Caligula desired, but, owing to modern progress, they are not thought to be mad. There is a near and imminent prospect that other countries will soon possess H-bombs. France and Germany want them. We must suppose that China will soon think they are necessary. Can we doubt that Egypt and Israel will demand 'the great deterrent'? Unless measures are taken very soon, every Sovereign State will soon possess H-bombs.

This will enormously increase the likelihood of the Great Powers being drawn into war against their will. It is both our duty and our interest to prevent the acquisition of H-bombs by Powers which do not yet possess them. For this reason, if for no other reason, Great Britain ought to renounce H-bombs and do everything in its power to cause Russia and America to prevent their acquisition by any State which does not yet have them. It would not be at all difficult for Russia and America, if they were in agreement, to secure this result, and such co-operation might be the beginning of better relations.

Nuclear weapons must be abandoned everywhere

The talk of the 'great deterrent' is plain nonsense. Those who use this argument always go on to say that of course it will not be necessary to actually employ the deterrent. But, if this were really believed, it is obvious that each side would be willing to agree to its abolition. It is, in fact, a futile weapon, since it will destroy those who use it as well as those against whom it is used. There should be an agreement to destroy all stocks of nuclear weapons and to submit to neutral inspection to make sure that the agreement is observed.

Negotiations for a detente should be entered into

All negotiations in recent years have been more or less insincere. The aim on each side has not been to reach agreement, but to make proposals which are good for propaganda purposes and involve concealed advantages for one's own side. What is needed is a new direction on both sides and a determination, not only to make proposals, but to find compromises which give no net advantage to either side. We are constantly told that there is a risk in negotiating with the Soviet Government. But those who say this overlook the risk involved in not negotiating. The risk involved in not negotiating is the extermination of the human race. This, surely, is a greater risk than that of some diplomatic advantage to one side or the other. We must hope that this will become obvious both to Russia and to the United States. Each side should abandon abuse of the other side. We are all sinners. No Great Power has the right to cast the first stone. What is needed on both sides is emphasis on our common interest in human survival rather than upon the matters in which our interests are supposed to differ. Whether we wish it or not, the only road to the welfare of each is the welfare of all."

[Synopsis of Bertrand Russell's Speech,
procured by Gerald Holtom, 1958]

At the end of the meeting, Canon Collins suggested that anyone who wished to take a petition to No.10 Downing Street could do so then and there. The audience had been captivated and profoundly moved by the speeches. Gerald recalls:

"Many of us wandered off to Downing Street, no shouting or noise, more like a church congregation released after two hours of prayers and sermons. Perhaps there were 500 people or more in Downing Street. Suddenly there were dark blue police vans and police with alsatian dogs barking and running about. I saw one man being dragged by his feet by two policemen and his head was scraped along the pavement. I was pushed in the back and so was my friend's wife. So we went back home to Twickenham."

He was irritated by an article in one of the leading newspapers that referred to the gathering as 'communist rabble' and went to see their editorial staff to protest, saying that:

"Here was the most important issue of the day discussed by some of the most respected and erudite elders of our century being entirely ignored."

Gerald wrote to some of the speakers present at the CND meeting, asking for written copies of their speeches so that they could be circulated around schools for educational purposes. It turned out that many of them had been improvised or were unobtainable. Bertrand Russell kindly sent a copy of his speech that has been used in this chapter.

The question now was how would humanity be persuaded to acquiesce to its own survival?

London to Aldermaston

The Direct Action Committee Against Nuclear War (DAC) were in the process of organising a protest march against the H-bomb. Gerald wanted to offer his services and went to their *Peace News* office in London, where he met Michael Randle, Hugh Brock and Pat Arrowsmith. He asked them about the march and was told that it was going to leave Trafalgar Square on Good Friday and go to Aldermaston, about 52 miles in total. *"Four days at Easter whatever the weather"*, they said, *"from London to the Atomic Weapons Research Establishment (AWRE)."*

Gerald was impressed by their intuitive intent and reassurance. Hugh Brock had been the editor of *Peace News* since 1951. He had also been a member of the Non Violent Resistance Group (NVR) which stemmed from the Peace Pledge Union. They had all been inspired by the Quakers' philosophy of pacifism and by Mahatma Gandhi. The NVR protested against Britain's decision to manufacture atomic weapons and had demonstrated in front of the War Office, in January 1952, and three months later at the AWRE in Aldermaston. Two thousand women had marched from Hyde Park to Trafalgar Square, on 12 May 1957, to demonstrate against the H-bomb, while Harold Steele was trying to prevent nuclear testing in the Pacific. All these events had helped to arouse public opinion against the H-bomb, but it was still not enough to make the British government change its mind. Those who had supported Harold Steele's venture and the NVR demonstrations had met in London in November 1957 and had decided to organise a protest march to the AWRE.

The DAC was set up *'to assist the conducting of nonviolent direct action to obtain the total renunciation of nuclear war and its weapons by Britain and all other countries as a first step in disarmament.'* They were also prepared to resort to civil disobedience if necessary. Their policy statement read:

'Weapons for mass destruction threaten to deprive millions of people of the most fundamental of all human rights; the right to live. Reliance on the H-bomb is therefore quite incompatible with democracy, and it is

our duty to oppose it by every nonviolent means in our power, even if it means unconstitutional action. When the powers of the constitution itself are used to bolster up policies that are basically undemocratic then civil disobedience is imperative.'

The 1958 protest march from London to Aldermaston was going to focus attention on the centre of Britain's nuclear weapons programme. Gerald asked if he could help the DAC with the organisation of the march by designing the visual effects, with banners of some sort which could be clearly seen and photographed by the press. They did not know how many people would turn up, but publicity and support for the march had already been given by CND at their inaugural meeting and the numbers might be high, perhaps several thousand. The DAC agreed to Gerald's proposals and they arranged another meeting to see what he could come up with.

Gerald was an established self-employed artist specialising in textile appliqué. His workshop was in Twickenham, London, where he designed and made large proscenium curtains for schools and wall hangings for new churches. He had recently completed a design for the chancel in St. Oswald's Church in Coventry, which had been commissioned by Sir Basil Spence. His work involved a certain amount of research into mythology and symbolism. He began to think about a design that could be used for the Aldermaston march. His first thoughts focused on some form of the Christian cross, associated in his mind with the early Christian teachings of nonviolence and pacifism.

Gerald began by painting white discs on black squares which were filled in with different forms of the Christian cross. After discussing his ideas with various people he began to have doubts about using the cross motif: *'There followed the realisation in my mind that the crusaders had used the cross in Malta, the Victoria Cross in Britain, the Iron Cross in Germany and the Croix de Guerre in France, together with the awful fact that the Christian cross in 1958 was associated in the public mind throughout the world with the manufacture, testing and blessing of the atomic bomb.'* Further research added to Gerald's misgivings: *'In a hasty survey, all the church leaders who I interviewed refused point blank to associate their religions with this march project. The Christian cross, which was prolific in my original sketch, was therefore eliminated.'*

Gerald arranged a meeting with Reverend Davis from Twickenham to see if he had any ideas on the subject. He was a kind enthusiastic man who suggested making placards with a white dove on a black background, surrounded by flames. Gerald thanked him for his thoughts and went home to produce seven different designs. However, the dove motif also turned out to be inappropriate; somebody had pointed out that Picasso's painting of a dove had been adopted by the Communist Party.

Gerald was profoundly disturbed by the fact that the atomic bomb had been made and used by a society to which he himself belonged. He drew onto his sketchbook late into the night, alienated and distressed. A shape began to take form. It was intuitive:

'That night I drew myself, doodled on the page, in the formalised motif of a man in despair, and put a circle around it which represented the world, planet Earth, with one little man in despair upon it. Despair was triggered off in my own mind and that of many others, at the realisation that the idea of unilateral nuclear disarmament, leading to unilateral disarmament, ran contrary to almost all established political systems and religions.'

Retrospectively, the despair gesture reminded him of an illustration made by Francisco Goya, possibly from *The Disasters of War* series, 1810-20. One of the prints shows a peasant kneeling with arms outstretched downwards in deep despair, protesting against war.

Gerald had now drawn the despair motif but the concept of nuclear disarmament had to be justified somehow. He was familiar with the international semaphore signals, which use two hand-held flags in various positions, to spell out messages from boats at sea. Fortunately, these signals provided a solution:

'The problem of justifying this symbol was resolved when I began to analyse the origin of the despair gesture with both arms outstretched downwards. Obviously such gestures predated alphabets. I turned to semaphore signals and found that this gesture stood for N and that the vertical line, with one arm down and the other arm up, stood for D. So here I had justification for the ND symbol, the Nuclear Disarmament Symbol.

Another important concept was still missing and that was unilateralism. Gerald realised shortly afterwards that by turning the ND Symbol upside down, the upward outstretched lines and the vertical line could represent U and D, in semaphore signalling, and therefore Unilateral Disarmament. This reversed form of the symbol could also represent the tree of life and a symbol for hope. Gerald imagined that "*a 'revolution of thought' might*

*Gerald's painting of the Nuclear Disarmament Symbol,
combining the semaphore letters N and D, 1958*

One of Gerald's preliminary sketches for the demonstration, 1958

take place during the march, from the rule by force of armaments to the concept of nonviolence... from despair to the realisation that the answer lies within the grasp of each individual; Unilateral Disarmament. If the individual disarms himself he no longer constitutes a threat."

The symbol could now be explained but its meaning was not immediately obvious. Gerald got round this problem by associating the symbol with slogans on banners that related to nuclear disarmament and non-violence that would qualify its meaning during the four day march. He had also thought of using the international code flags for the letters N and D, which were shown in his preliminary sketches, but this idea was abandoned. The validity and certainty of this symbol was now fixed in Gerald's mind. He wanted to make it clear that:

'This symbol was never intended as a shorthand mark for a collection of words or prayers, or as a substitute for action. Nor was the symbol intended to be used like a flag or badge by which a political or religious group can be recognised. The ND Symbol was designed as an individual and personal witness of a train of thought upon the subject of war and peace, death and life.' He went on to say: *'The responsibility of the individual was to be virtually the signature tune of the first Aldermaston march. Responsibility of the individual is a concept often beyond comprehension and seldom put into practice.'*

Gerald presented his ideas to the Direct Action Committee on 21 February 1958. He showed them his drawings of marchers holding banners and placards and explained how his symbol could represent unilateral nuclear disarmament. They approved of his ideas and Gerald was requisitioned to design and make the visual display equipment for the London to Aldermaston march. He did not make a copyright of the Peace Symbol; the concept of unilateral nuclear disarmament was far beyond the realms of commercial interest.

First of all, Gerald went to Trafalgar Square to take measurements. He wanted to get an idea of the size of lettering for banners that could be easily read and photographed from the plinth of Nelson's Column, or from the steps in front of the National Gallery. He also thought about the size and number of individually hand held ND Symbols that would be practical and effective. The plan was to make 500 discs of the ND Symbol, attached to short wooden laths, for people to carry on the march. There would be 250 with white on a black background for Good Friday and Saturday, and 250 with Green on white for Easter Sunday and Monday, marking the

▲ *Gerald's daughter Anna with a friend making ND 'lollipops', 1958*

▼ *Gerald's 'banner wagon' on the left, Twickenham, 1958*

transition from winter to spring and from death to life.

Gerald took his drawing to a local screen printer and ordered 500 sheets of paper with the ND Symbol printed on one half, and the words Nuclear Disarmament on the other half. He then cut two corrugated cardboard discs 16 inches in diameter and glued them together on the end of a wooden lath that had been bought from a builders' merchant, so as to sandwich the lath between the two discs. The rectangular screen print was then folded in half and glued over the cardboard discs with waterproof glue and trimmed into a circle. They were made in Gerald's workshop in Twickenham with help from his family and friends, and became affectionately known as 'lollipops'.

Several long banners were made by sewing together offcut strips of shiny black Italian cloth. They were 22 feet long and 16 inches high. The lettering was painted on with white emulsion paint and lengths of nylon string were sewn into the top and bottom hems and attached to wooden poles. The poles were cut to three different lengths: nine, eight and seven feet long. The banners were going to be set out in three concentric semicircles in Trafalgar Square and their different heights would enable them to be photographed simultaneously from the plinth at Nelson's Column.

The slogans read:

UNILATERAL NUCLEAR DISARMAMENT

NO H-BOMBS FOR BRITAIN

FIRST STEP TO PEACE

AGAINST ALL BOMBS BRITAIN USA AND USSR

FROM FEAR TO SANITY

MAKE FRIENDS NOT ENEMIES

NUCLEAR DISARMAMENT

NO MISSILE BASES HERE

WOULD YOU DROP THE BOMB?

Each slogan began and ended with the ND Symbol.

Gerald rigged up a banner for his VW minibus which later became known as the 'banner wagon'. Steel tubes were welded onto brackets and mounted onto each bumper. A banner could then be flown fore and aft between them, clear above the roof rack, proclaiming Nuclear Disarmament, in bright white emulsion, complete with the ND Symbol at each end. This resulted in requests from at least 25 private car owners for similar equipment, the first being a Putney Borough Councilor, Mrs. Anne Clark, who turned up at Gerald's workshop to have her car modified and revolutionised, all for a good cause.

Gerald's textile appliqué workshop was now used exclusively for producing display material for the Aldermaston march. He was helped by two machinists and another artist, David Holt. The sewing machines ran flat out for days on end; there was one used for fine zigzag stitching and another for fast sewing.

Michael Howard turned up in the workshop one day to see how things were going. He was a DAC member and the chief marshal for the Aldermaston march. He thought it would be good to include three large main banners with the inscription 'March from London to Aldermaston'. One for the lead, one in the middle and one at the tail end of the march. There might be a big turnout. They would also be needing a number of armbands for his marshals, each with a particular colour for a specific job; red and white for marshals looking after groups of people and black and white for those holding the banners. He asked Gerald if he could make this equipment and take charge of the delivery, distribution and collection of the banners with the use of his 'banner wagon', which he willingly agreed to.

The main banners were framed with aluminium tubing and carried in shoulder slings by two marchers. Strings attached to the top corners of the frames, held by people walking fore and aft, could maintain the structure in a vertical position if necessary. Gerald sewed pockets onto these banners for flowers. He also incorporated two ND Symbols made with gold leaf that flashed in the light beside the lettering.

Gerald was still loading up the van with banners, 'lollipops' and armbands at three o'clock in the morning, with the help of his friend Michael Bruce. It was 4 April, 1958, the first day of the London to Aldermaston march. After a short night's sleep he set off on a long eerie drive through the streets of London to Trafalgar Square. There was nobody there except for three motorcycle police and one inspector with a flat peaked hat. Gerald parked his van beside the plinth at Nelson's Column

The three main banners on the plinth of Nelson's Column, 1958 ▶

▲ *Gerald holding flowers with the main banner, helped by his son Ben in the foreground. Pat Arrowsmith talks with Hugh Brock on the left, Traflagar Square, 1958*

▲ *Trafalgar Square, 4 April 1958*
▼ *Gerald distributes ND 'lollipops' to marchers, Trafalgar Square, 1958*

and asked the inspector if he thought anyone would turn up. He was a friendly man and looked at Gerald's black armband with the white lettering 'banner marshal' written on it. "Well, it doesn't start until eleven," he replied.

The first long banner was unfurled and stretched tight. People started drifting into Trafalgar Square. Volunteers took hold of each pole and the words MAKE FRIENDS NOT ENEMIES could be clearly read. Helpers appeared from everywhere and soon 25 long banners were laid out in semi circles on the ground. A crowd was beginning to gather, then the Twickenham banner appeared with a group of friends and their children, displaying a large painting of a man and a woman holding a child. This was the only figurative design that was displayed on the march, which had been painted by Madeleine. It symbolised humanity and life for future generations.

Three of Gerald's children, Julia, Anna and Ben, who was now thirteen, helped to assemble the main banners with their friends and set them up on the plinth of Nelson's Column. A few 'lollipops' were handed out displaying the ND Symbol and the plinth became full of photographers. The banners could be easily read from the National Gallery steps. Gerald asked the police inspector how many people he thought were there. "About ten thousand," he replied. Pat Arrowsmith and Hugh Brock appeared from amidst the crowd, smiling but pensive.

The meeting in Trafalgar square began with one minute's silence. It was to be an act of repentance by each participant for the suffering caused by the atomic bombings of Hiroshima and Nagasaki and a dedication to the struggle against further use and production of atomic weapons. After the silence, loudspeakers crackled and Bayard Rustin spoke, followed by an impassioned speech from Harold Steele. Bayard Rustin was well known in the United States both as a pacifist and for his work in race relations. During the war he had been imprisoned for three years as a conscientious objector and later helped Martin Luther King with the twelve month boycott in Montgomery, Alabama, which led to racial integration on the city's buses. His first words spoken from the plinth of Nelson's column were: *"We are non-violent because injury to one is injury to all"*.

Michael Howard took the microphone and gave instructions of how the march was going to proceed. The leading banner set off from the south west corner of Trafalgar Square, followed by people walking four abreast. Gerald handed out more black and white 'lollipops' as the procession advanced, the idea being to distribute 250 over the whole length of the march. When this had been done he drove to the front of the march at the

Royal Albert Hall where he took some photographs. By the time the last main banner had left Trafalgar Square, the leading banner was approaching Exhibition Road. Lawrence Brown led the way with his measured tread and stopwatch. He was one of the NVR members who had helped organise previous demonstrations at Aldermaston, Porton and Mildenhall bomber base.

Gerald thought the march looked quite dignified. He saw one policeman, finely mounted on horseback, and two police motorcyclists. The marshals were amateur platoon sergeants who looked after small groups of people and kept them informed about accommodation arrangements, food and medical aid. They were linked to their chief marshal Michael Howard in his caravan office, known as the co-op van. Somebody had kindly agreed to drive Gerald's 'banner wagon' to Hounslow, which was the destination for the first day, leaving him free to walk on the march. After a halt at Turnham Green, Gerald was curious to see how heavy the leading banner was. His daughter Julia, who had been carrying the banner with a retired man in his early seventies, was reluctant to give it up even to the one who made it and wanted to test it!

▼ *Demonstrators in London on their way to Aldermaston, 1958*

Foul weather had been forecast for Saturday, the second day of the march. Gerald was up early and drove to Hounslow with his children and a thermos full of hot soup. Snowflakes began to obscure the windscreen as they reached Bell Corner on Hounslow Broadway. The march set off at 10 o'clock and headed towards Maidenhead via Colnbrook and Slough. Pat Arrowsmith had replaced Michael Howard as chief marshal and gave instructions through the loudspeaker of the co-op van. The leading banner began to move and a column of people formed and followed. Numbers dropped to about 600, all very wet. The road towards Slough was inches deep in snow and there was a cold headwind laden with sleet. Bank Holiday cars came sweeping by, sometimes dangerously close, drenching the marchers with slush from the dirty road. Fortunately the 'lollipops' were conspicuous and served as good signaling devices to ward off the traffic.

Despite the bad weather, Julia and her fellow marcher managed to carry the leading banner. They passed London Airport and by midday a thousand more people had joined the demonstration. The weary marchers eventually reached Maidenhead where they stopped for the night and slept in school halls, huddled together on the floors in their sleeping bags. Animated conversations took place despite their exhaustion. The rain soaked banners were collected up and stored in the 'banner wagon' ready for the next day.

Easter Sunday looked promising. There was even sunshine and many more people turned up. Gerald filled the pockets of the three main banners with bunches of spring flowers that he had picked from his garden. There were daffodils, Japonica, lilies, tulips and forsythia. He then distributed the green and white 'lollipops' displaying the ND Symbol to mark the change from winter to spring. The march left Maidenhead station yard at 10 o'clock and went to Reading via Knowl Hill. Jazz bands played and people sang and danced along the way as the number of participants increased to about 6000.

ND Symbols began to appear in the windows of some of the houses. Gerald had supplied people with car banners, stickers and badges for use on the march. He produced 10 inch square prints for window display and 20 inch square prints for poster banners, all in a variety of colours: red, blue, green, purple, black and yellow. The ND Symbol was beginning to take on a new significance. Real hospitality was found in those houses displaying it; the marchers were offered tea and sandwiches and a floor to sleep on if necessary. The ND Symbol stuck on a car meant the driver would stop and offer a lift to a hitchhiker and the ND Symbol shown on a haversack meant the hiker was good for a lift.

When the march came to a halt for the afternoon break, Gerald noticed a large tea urn with two brass handles being taken off a van by a man wearing a long overcoat and a peaked cap. He took one handle and helped the man carry the urn up a path to a house, where they were ushered into a kitchen by a friendly matron and a group of enthusiastic young people. Their eyes beamed with delight as they topped up the urn with boiling water from kettles and saucepans. They were Russian students who were staying for a few months in England and the matron was their housekeeper. As they struggled with the urn back to the grass verge, now full of tea, the sight of their astonishment and pleasure at seeing the extent of the march remained fixed in Gerald's mind. In the evening, once again, school floors were turned into heaps of sleeping bodies of all ages, some with sleeping bags or makeshift coverings, with haversacks for pillows.

On Easter Monday the marchers reassembled at St. Mary's Butts in Reading for the final leg to Aldermaston. Most of the people who came out to watch appeared astonished. A young woman with a baby waved happily from the window of her house. One of the most heartening episodes took place when a large column of people from the West Country turned up. Before long, the Atomic Weapons Research Establishment loomed up ahead. The marchers walked in silence beside the perimeter fence and spiralled slowly into Falcon Field where they planted the leading banner in the grass. Gerald looked at the cluster of buildings behind the barbed wire. It was here that a hydrogen bomb had been made and detonated over Christmas Island the year before. It was here that more hydrogen bombs were being made. Gerald's gaze turned to the bunch of flowers in the main banner and he thought to himself: *'what is the use of trying to oppose nuclear weapons with a bunch of flowers?'*

Despite Gerald's feeling of helplessness, the united support of people sharing widely differing political and religious views made this Aldermaston march a powerful protest against the manufacture of the H-bomb in Britain. The demonstration had cornered the main press coverage for four days and a documentary film had been made by Lindsay Anderson and Karel Reisz: *'March to Aldermaston'*. Many of the participants took their 'lollipops' displaying *'Nuclear Disarmament'* back to their homes, some as far away as New Zealand, Canada and Japan. The seeds of peace had been sown. Gerald hoped that his little symbol would be remembered among the myriads of truth. He also noted: *'During my life, the maximum effort of endurance and endeavour which I have achieved was the preparation and organisation of the visual effects of the first Aldermaston march.'*

Aldermaston and beyond

The 1958 London to Aldermaston protest march against nuclear weapons marked the beginning of a series of similar marches that took place each year at Easter, which became collectively known as the 'Aldermaston marches'. From 1959 onwards they were organised by CND, with Canon Collins leading the way, and went from Aldermaston to London. The number of participants grew each year and attracted many international contingents, including people from Japan. The last of these 80 km marches, in 1963, drew together an estimated 100,000 people.

Gerald participated in the Aldermaston marches for five consecutive years and provided visual display material up until 1961. He was impressed by some ceramic ND badges that had been made by the artist Eric Austen in 1959 for CND. His findings added another powerful interpretation of Gerald's original design. Gerald noted:

'Immediately following the first march, an ND badge version of the symbol was devised and made by Eric Austen who made small ceramic white discs on which he painted the form of the symbol in black slip, fired them in his own kiln and fixed pins to the reverse side with adhesive. The result was a refinement of craftsmanship of the highest standard. Furthermore, Eric Austen's research into the origins of symbolism confirmed that the gesture of despair motif has been associated through ancient history with the death of man, and the circle with the unborn child. The significance of the two motifs combined is the predicament in which, by chance, we live.'

The peace movement intensified not only in Britain, but all over the world as East West relations deteriorated in the Cold War, with the crisis over Berlin, the establishment of nuclear missile bases and ongoing nuclear testing.

In November 1959 DAC members were making plans for a protest entry into the French atomic testing area in the Sahara Desert. The protest was sponsored by the Ghana Council for Nuclear Disarmament and the

American Committee for Nonviolent Action. They intended to give leaflets to the workmen and technicians preparing for the nuclear test in Reggane, Algeria, in order to dissuade them from continuing. Should their attempts fail, they would be ready to stay in the area and risk injury or death from the explosion and fallout and, by doing so, show the rest of the world the terrible consequences of an atomic bomb. However, the test took place sooner than expected, on 13 February 1960. Canon Collins and Bertrand Russell delivered a protest letter to the French Embassy a week after the explosion.

Directly after the 1960 Aldermaston march, Gerald was one of a handful of marchers from Twickenham who attempted to carry one of the leading banners, proclaiming nuclear disarmament, on from Trafalgar Square to the summit meeting in Paris (called to address the worsening situation in Berlin), via Canterbury, Dover and Calais. Other organisations would then hopefully be able to take the banner in relays to Geneva, Vienna, Prague and possibly Moscow. However, after their ferry crossing to Calais they were courteously but firmly halted by the French Police. The banner was locked up in a police station near the Place de Crèvecoeur in Calais, with a bunch of lilies of the valley in its pocket. The flowers had been picked on 1 May, ironically the same day the Soviets shot down an American spy plane flying over their country; the summit conference planned for 17 May 1960, to ease tensions in the Cold War, ended in failure.

Frustrations were building up as Bertrand Russell resigned from his presidency with CND to form the 'Committee of 100', on 22 October 1960. This alternative peace movement comprised a hundred eminent signatories including Reverend Michael Scott. They believed that nonviolent civil disobedience was now necessary in order to achieve nuclear disarmament. Many of its members had also been members of the Direct Action Committee; Michael Randle was now their secretary. The Committee of 100 organised their first sit-down demonstration in front of the Ministry of Defence in London on 18 February 1961. The date coincided with the arrival of the *Proteus*, an American supply ship for Polaris nuclear submarines, on the River Clyde in Scotland. Michael Randle asked Gerald if he could make a large banner for the protest demonstration, which he did. It displayed 'Action for life' and incorporated four ND Symbols, one in each corner of the rectangle.

Gerald's commitment to the peace movement was beginning to have an effect on his family life and may have contributed to his domestic crisis on 19 February 1961, when Madeleine said that she was going to move out. Their marriage ended in divorce shortly after. 1961 was a particularly turbulent year. Peace organisations converged, merged and diverged, in a desperate attempt to arouse people's conscience and bring an end to the arms race and an end to war. During the Aldermaston march that year, Gerald was one of the marshals responsible for some of the international contingents who came from Norway, Sweden, Denmark, Belgium and Switzerland. Through his contacts with Reverend Davies, 80 marchers were able to have accommodation at St. Mary's Hall in Twickenham. About 25 or so were hosted by Gerald at his home. Between 40,000 and 50,000 people marched through to Trafalgar Square on Easter Monday that year.

The Committee of 100 organised another mass civil disobedience sit-down in London's Parliament Square on 29 April 1961, in an attempt to bring a halt to the nuclear arms race. Attention was drawn to the Polaris submarines skirting the Russian coast and the crisis over Berlin that could sweep the world into a nuclear war. Over 800 people were arrested during the demonstration, including Gerald, who was fined one pound at Bow Street Magistrates' Court for obstructing the streets. Gerald noted afterwards: *'We, the protesters, commonly identified in the National Press as 'nuclear squatters', supported by the Committee of 100 and by many respected living prophets and philosophers of our time, including Bertrand Russell, were prevented by police from stating our case in Parliament Square.'*

The Direct Action Committee organised a 545 mile march from London to Scotland on Easter Monday 1961, directly after the Aldermaston march, carrying a banner displaying 'Polaris Protest' with an ND Symbol on each side of the wording. They arrived seven weeks later and about 2,000 people joined the final lap of the march from Dunoon to Holy Loch. The protest began on Sunday 21 May. Demonstrators left from both sides of Holy Loch in a flotilla of small boats and attempted to board Polaris vessels in the harbour. Gerald had hoped to be able to supply a boat for the demonstration but the strains of direct action were beginning to show. He wrote at the time: *'I must admit that I am too exhausted by work which I am committed to do to cope with the elaborate job of getting the boat to Scotland ... I am in the position of providing for a large family and subscribing to charity to a certain extent. It is impossible to work full time for direct action.'* Demonstrators at Holy Loch attempted to occupy Ardnadam Pier that was used by the crew of the *Proteus* and the nuclear submarines. 43 demonstrators were arrested and received fines and prison sentences. The DAC decided to disband and merged with the Committee of 100 in June 1961. In September 1961 the Committee of 100 organised two simultaneous demonstrations, one at the Polaris base in Scotland and another in Parliament Square in London. Prior to the demonstration, Bertrand Russell, at the age of 89, was imprisoned for refusing not to incite the public to civil disobedience.

Members of the American Committee for Nonviolent Action (CNVA) were in the process of walking from San Francisco to Moscow, a distance of 6,000 miles, protesting against the armaments of the East and West. They passed through England on their way in June 1961. The CNVA had close links with the British pacifist movement and had adopted the ND Symbol for their leaflets and placards. Gerald was invited by Hugh Brock to meet some of their members at Friends House, London, on 2 June 1961. He would also be able to meet people from Britain who were helping to organise this *'imaginative attempt to unify and stimulate support for unilateral disarmament in a number of countries in both Western and Eastern Europe.'* On Sunday 4 June 1961, the CNVA march leader, Bradford Lyttle, spoke to a crowd of 6,000 people at a send-off rally in Trafalgar Square organised by CND. The marchers walked to Aldermaston where they held a three hour vigil and spoke to the workers. On 10 June they held another vigil outside the Greenham Common US airbase before going on to Southampton. The team was refused entry to France at the port of Le Havre and after a second attempt, involving a spectacular jump into the sea from the ferry by one of their members, they went on their way via Belgium. Their passage through England was particularly significant and marked the transition from an all-American project to an international one. British and Scandinavian volunteers joined the march and supported a venture that was taking the message of unilateral disarmament into the Communist countries. The team passed through West and East Germany and reached Red Square in Moscow on 3 October 1961, leaving the Berlin Wall behind them.

The ND Symbol spread rapidly to the US after the first Aldermaston march in 1958, largely through the influence of the American pacifist Bayard Rustin and the CNVA, where it was used by anti-nuclear and anti-war organisations, and also by the civil rights movement. Within weeks, Albert Bigelow, who was a member of the CNVA, flew a flag displaying the ND Symbol from the masthead of his boat, *Golden Rule,* during his attempts to stop US nuclear testing in the Marshall Islands.

Once the ND Symbol had left the sphere of the Aldermaston marches and spread to other countries, it became known as the 'Peace Symbol'. It was displayed at open air rock concerts in the USA at the height of 'flower power' in the 1960s and widely used for protesting against the Vietnam

War. Anti-draft demonstrators displayed the American flag with the Peace Symbol replacing the stars on the flag. Students from the North High School in Des Moines, Iowa, wore black armbands with a white Peace Symbol as a protest against the conflict in Vietnam; they were suspended from class and their case was taken to the Supreme Court in 1969. On 4 May 1970, four students at Kent State University in Ohio were shot and killed by National Guardsmen for demonstrating against President Nixon's decision to invade Cambodia. This tragedy, combined with the tragedy of the war, provoked widespread protest demonstrations across the country in which the Peace Symbol was always present.

The Peace Symbol soon became associated with the protection of the natural environment and one of the most important organisations to emerge from the peace movement relating to this was *Greenpeace*. Their campaigning against nuclear weapons and against nuclear power stations, while promoting renewable energy systems, corresponded entirely with Gerald's philosophy. They made some badges with a green Peace Symbol that included a small yellow circle with a horizontal line through the middle. The yellow motif combined the letters 'e' for Earth and 'o' for the organisms that call it home. The badges were sold to help raise funds for their first protest demonstration in 1971 when they attempted to sail to Amchitka Island in Alaska, where the US was planning to carry out nuclear tests. It was a protest against the ecological damage that the nuclear tests were doing to the fragile Arctic ecosystem and against nuclear weapons. Further demonstrations against French nuclear testing in the Pacific Ocean led to the sabotage of the Greenpeace vessel, *Rainbow Warrior*, on 10 July 1985, by French secret agents in Auckland harbour, New Zealand. The explosion sank the vessel and caused the tragic death of the Greenpeace photographer, Fernando Pereira. The sailing ship was later replaced by another *Rainbow Warrior* that had a large Peace Symbol painted on its deck.

Some of the most dedicated and courageous demonstrations against nuclear war were made by 'women for life on earth' at Greenham Common in Berkshire, which became a focal point of anti-nuclear activity in Britain throughout the 1980s. They were protesting against Britain's agreement with the US to install 96 nuclear-armed cruise missiles at the American airbase at Greenham Common that would effectively make Britain the front line in the event of a nuclear war between eastern and western powers. The women camped in makeshift tents in harsh conditions around the nine mile perimeter fence of the American airbase in a demonstration that lasted nineteen years. During this time they covered the fence with all kinds of objects and artwork that expressed their fears and hopes for the future. Gerald went to visit them on occasions and gave his encouragement. The Peace Symbol would often be included on their banners, alongside or linked to another symbol comprising a circle with a crossed vertical line beneath it, to represent women for peace.

Since the day Gerald drew his three lines in a circle, the Peace Symbol has been used by countless people around the world. You might see it chalked on a pavement, marked in the snow, scratched in the sand, or displayed on a piece of jewelry … compelling and obscure. Despite some of its frivolous use in the fashion industry, the Peace Symbol has essentially retained its original, profound significance. It has become part of a universal consciousness. Australian aboriginals have painted the Peace Symbol on their faces while protesting against uranium mining on their territory in 1985. The Peace Symbol has been widely used to protest against nuclear power stations which have inevitably led to numerous accidents and long-term ecological damage such as the nuclear disaster at Chernobyl in 1986, Fukushima in 2011 and half a century of radioactive waste dumped at sea.

An estimated two million people took to the streets in London in 2003 to protest against the war in Iraq, the largest anti-war demonstration ever held in Britain, where the Peace Symbol was widely used.

In 2022 the peace symbol has been combined with the yellow and blue of the Ukrainian flag as a protest against the invasion and bombing of Ukraine by Russian forces.

Screen Printing and Textile Appliqué

After the Second World War, Gerald moved with his wife Madeleine and their four children to Grosvenor House in Twickenham in London. He established himself as a self- employed artist under the name of *Gerald Holtom Ltd* and set up a workshop in part of the house for making theatre curtains and printed textiles. Gerald was inspired by the work of several well-known artists who experimented with textile printing at that time, such as Henry Moore, John Piper, John Farleigh and Graham Sutherland. He particularly liked the natural shapes of plant growth and roots that were shown in some of their prints.

The microscopic life forms that drift in suspension through the oceans of the world were another great source of inspiration. Gerald made a design called *Plankton* for the Festival of Britain in 1951 which was displayed at the Dome of Discovery in London. This textile wall covering was a screen print showing various magnified forms of radiolaria. These microorganisms are a particular kind of zooplankton which have beautifully shaped siliceous structures resembling stars or sea urchins. He printed his design onto cotton in a variety of colours. An example of his work is kept at the Victoria and Albert Museum.

From 1950 to 1970 Gerald was commissioned by the Ministry of Education to make proscenium curtains for post-war schools, using his own particular technique of textile appliqué. Subjects often reflected Britain's cultural and industrial past. He was also commissioned by architects, private companies and institutions to make curtains, wall hangings and murals. They covered large wall areas and included wall hangings for modern post-war churches. When he employed assistants, he always tried to encourage their creative flare. David Holt was an artist from Kent who worked with him on several designs.

Gerald described his textile appliqué *'as being similar to tapestry in so far as the finished product serves the same purpose. Where tapestry tends to be a reproduction of a painting or cartoon, my own brands of textile appliqué are as direct as a painting. The artist is involved with drawing, cutting out and the precise selection of colour and texture, as well as the*

'Plankton' screen print, designed by Gerald Holtom, 1951

handling of diverse materials. I usually work on heavy linens and sometimes on nets to which I apply all manner of materials including cotton, prints, wool, silk and 4mm plywood that can be painted or stained. I also use leather that is sometimes coated with gold or silver leaf. I "draw" lines with wool yarns stitched to the material.'

Gerald and his associates exhibited three samples of their proscenium curtains and wall hangings at the Building Centre in Store Street, London, in January 1957. One of these textile appliqué designs, *'Hatfield House'*, was 12ft high and 40ft in length. It showed a whole set of architectural facades with vivid red and white brickwork and masonry that contrasted with the blue sky. The sky itself was enriched with Jacobean patterns that appeared beneath the printing dye. This work had been made for a school in Hatfield, Hertfordshire. Another mural showed a number of Shakespearean characters, commissioned for a school in Sheffield. The third design depicted the baptism of St. Alban, based on illustrations from a thirteenth century manuscript, made for St. Albans Primary School in Holborn, London.

The *'Seven Pillars of Education'* were made for a school in Staffordshire, which included large portraits of Queen Elizabeth the First and Comenius, commissioned by Frank Rutter in 1958.

The *'Hindu Dance'*, with Radha and peacocks, was a colourful textile appliqué displayed in the Jehangir Room at the Commonwealth Institute in London, commissioned by Sir Robert Matthew, Johnson Marshall & Partners in 1962.

Gerald was commissioned by the architect Sir Basil Spence to make the chancel wall hanging for St. Oswald's Church in Tile Hill, Coventry. This new church was consecrated in 1957. Two large figures, about twice life size, of St. Oswald and St. Aidan were portrayed, symbolising early Christianity in the seventh century in Britain.

A whole variety of scenes were made in textile appliqué for schools and institutions around the country that related to historical events, such as tin mining in Cornwall and Arkwright's inventions for textile processing in Derbyshire. The mechanical complexities of John Harrison's marine chronometer were exposed on another design, marked with black zigzag stitching and embellished with silver leaf.

In 1962 Gerald was invited back to the Royal College of Art to give talks about his work and assist students in their artistic profession. It was there that he met my mother, Charmian Fearnley, who was studying sculpture at the RCA. Charmian and Gerald later became married and they went to live in Hythe in Kent, opposite St. Leonard's church, not far

S.58.

"SNOWFLAKE" 42″ wide. 1 colour. [G. Holton, Twickenham.]

▲ *Gerald sitching wool yarns to create a figure in textile appliqué*

◄ *Snowflake design for a printed textile made by Gerald*

▲ 'Hatfield House' displayed at the Building Centre, London, 1957
▼ Gerald in his workshop making 'Seven Pillars of Education', Twickenham, 1958

▲ *'Hindu dance', Commonwealth Institute, London, 1962*
▼ *Gerald's preliminary sketches for a textile appliqué of John Harrison's marine chronometer*

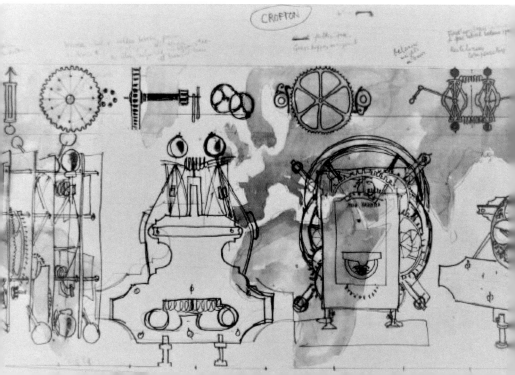

from the sea. My sister Rebecca was born in 1964 and I was born in 1966. My father continued to make textile appliqué designs at the family home in Hythe until his employment with the Ministry of Education came to an end. His last major job was a wall hanging for Tudor Hall in Barnet in 1969. This design was inspired by an Elizabethan pillow cover from the Victoria and Albert Museum, made in 1600, embroidered with biblical scenes. Gerald's textile appliqué was made from linen and worked in line drawings using red, black and grey wool yarns, silver leaf and machine stitching. There were various plants and animals, including a unicorn, with scenes of the flood and the plague, Noah's Ark and the Garden of Eden.

I still have vague memories of this wall hanging that was draped over the stairwell, before it was sent off to Barnet. The image of an elephant and a lion on their way to the Ark remains engraved in my mind. But above all I can remember the 'material cupboard'. This was a small storage space on the first floor of the house where my father kept rolls of printed cloth and cotton sacks full of material offcuts. It was a great place to hide for small children. Rebecca and I used to scramble inside the cupboard and delve into the sacks to see what we could find. A dusty beam of light from a chink in the door would reveal all kinds of treasures. There were mermaids, pieces of netting, plankton, horses, rabbits and architectural façades. If we searched long enough we would find tiny scraps of leather covered in gold and silver leaf that flashed in the semi-darkness.

◄ *Gerald points to a feature in his textile appliqué for a school in Pontefract, temporarily displayed in his garden in Twickenham*

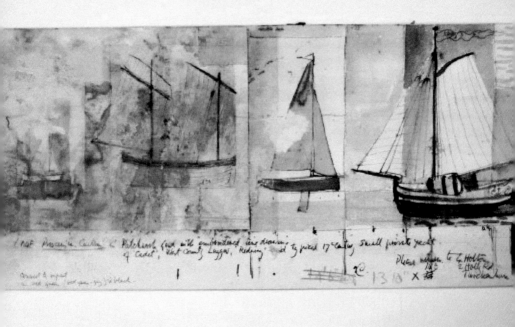

▲ *Gerald's preliminary sketches for a proscenium curtain design with sailing boats*

▼ *Gerald's preliminary sketches of figureheads*

The Foiler

After graduating from the Royal College of Art, my mother Charmian became established as a professional sculptress. She worked in her studio at the family home in Hythe and specialised in portrait heads which she modelled in clay. The sculptures were cast into bronze at a foundry or cast into Ciment Fondu by herself using Plaster of Paris moulds. She was commissioned to make a bronze head of the British tennis player Virginia Wade who won the women's singles championship at Wimbledon in 1977. Examples of her work are shown at the Metropole Arts Centre in Folkestone, which include a bronze head of its founder, Sir Gerald Glover. My mother made several portraits of Rebecca and myself as we changed from being toddlers to becoming teenagers. She would begin her work by building up layers of clay over a metal armature that was fixed to a wooden base. After careful observation of the model, she pressed on lumps of clay with her hands, using smaller and smaller pieces of clay as the work neared completion. From time to time she checked the dimensions of certain features with a pair of calipers. A nose would appear, then perhaps the mouth or an eye as the inert clay gradually came to life.

As young children Rebecca and I would happily sit for our mother in her studio while she made our portrait heads. When the session was over, or when we could no longer keep still, we would jump from the chair and run outside to explore the wild garden. We used to climb up the bay trees and the magnificent copper beech, or get tangled in the compact, bendy branches of the yew tree. Our father would be busy turning over the soil in the vegetable patch with a fork, sowing seeds or digging into the steaming compost heap. He grew all kinds of vegetables including carrots, potatoes, tomatoes, radishes, beans, sorrel and artichokes. If we foraged amongst the leaves we might even find some strawberries. Wood pigeons hooted from the tree tops, seagulls shrieked in the sky above and the clamour of the church bells marked the days.

My father had converted an old coach house into a workshop that was adjacent to the garden. On one particular occasion in the spring of 1971, I went to see what he was making. I had to tug hard and wrestle with the heavy concertina doors before they swung open. The air was tainted with the acrid smell of polyester resin. There before me was an orange boat, almost complete, in the shape of a kayak. She was named *Squid 1*. My father put down the 'wet and dry' carbon paper that he had been using for smoothing down the hull and hoisted me into the cockpit. I explored inside and crawled up to the bow, despite the tacky resin and the remains of fiberglass that made me itch. I was overjoyed by the thought that very soon we would be sailing out to sea.

Squid 1 was the first of a series of fast, innovative sailing boats with hydrofoils that my father had started to make in 1970. He called these prototypes *Foilers*. Gerald's passion for sailing had begun at the age of five when he first sailed to Blakeney Point in Norfolk. As a boy he loved to sail along the Norfolk coast and on the inland waters of the Broads, gradually learning the art of navigation with the local fishing community and from his own observations at sea. He soon became familiar with sea charts, tidal predictions and weather forecasts for planning his expeditions. A compass was used for setting a course or for taking bearings of prominent features to fix his position.

While he was working in London as a textile designer in the 1950s, he was never far from the wild creeks and the muddy banks of the Thames Estuary. Whenever the weather was fair and time permitted, he would escape from the city to sail on this vast natural outlet. As he navigated in the powerful currents he would often be accompanied by seabirds and a whole variety of vessels that entered and left the River Thames. On one occasion he sailed with his first wife Madeleine and two of their children, Peter and Julia, from Holehaven to Wivenhoe, on a small day boat called *Omega*. Sometimes he sailed alone from Burnham and explored the coast around Southend-on-Sea.

As well as these adventurous expeditions he also enjoyed the dinghy races that took place at Torquay in the English Channel. He used to go with his eldest son Peter to compete in the National 18ft Class. The conditions were often challenging. When the little boats ploughed through the trough of a wave their sails could disappear entirely from view.

One of Gerald's most intrepid voyages took him across the North Sea with two of his friends, Cecil and Terrence, from Faversham to Ostend, in July 1954. This was aboard Cecil's 23ft wooden sailing boat *Cleo*, built with carvel planking riveted to steamed oak frames. The hull was decked with plywood, leaving space for a small cockpit and a fore hatch. She was equipped with a Bermuda rig and a centreboard that could be pivoted.

Gerald's preliminary sketches of a Foiler ▶

▲ Gerald with one of his model Foilers at the gravel pit lake in Hythe
▼ Gerald working on his first prototype, 'Squid 1', in Hythe

After a certain amount of patching up and a coat of green paint, the boat was ready to sail. Green was the only colour they had, which was perhaps not the most auspicious colour to use at sea, but it would have to do. *Cleo* had been moored in Oare Creek at Faversham and as soon as the tide was on the ebb, Gerald and his friends hoisted the tan coloured foresail and pushed her off the mud into the narrow channel. With a south westerly breeze blowing and a favorable tidal stream, they raced past sandpipers and gulls that scavenged on the expanding mudflats. Before long the Isle of Sheppey appeared through the haze and they sailed eastwards along the coast to Whitstable, then on to Margate where they stopped for the night. In the morning they set sail on a compass course for the West Hinder Light-Ship in the North Sea. After passing a number of oil tankers and ferries on their way, they reached Ostend harbour late in the evening.

The design of an innovative sailing craft had been at the back of Gerald's mind since the 1960s. He had been particularly interested in an airborne lifeboat designed by Uffa Fox that could be easily beached on sand or shingle without the need for a harbour. Gerald's attention had also been drawn to some articles published by the Amateur Yacht Research Society between 1954 and 1968 that described experiments with surface piercing hydrofoils, made by Edmond Bruce and Dr John Morwood. Hydrofoils could be used to generate hydrodynamic forces that would counterbalance the capsizing effect of the wind on the sails of a boat, and also raise the hull vertically out of the water. There would be no need for a heavy keel or ballast and the wetted surface would be greatly reduced, enabling the boat to sail at high speed. Gerald had learnt some of the rudiments of naval architecture and was familiar with the handling and repair of small sailing boats and their components. He discussed with Dr Morwood how hydrofoils could be incorporated into outriggers, similar in arrangement to the traditional Polynesian fishing boats, and how they could be placed beneath the hull.

Gerald began to make drawings of *Foilers* with some of these ideas in mind. He then made some scaled models, complete with sails and hydrofoils that he tested on a gravel pit lake in Hythe. My mother took photographs and filmed while Rebecca and I watched excitedly as the little boats leapt to life and bounced over the ripples in a wake of spray, with their tiny leeward foil slicing through the water. Some of these models were exhibited at the London Boat Show in Earl's Court in January 1971. His initial design was intended for recreational purposes but he also had visions of its possible use as a cross channel ferry.

Gerald then made a series of full size prototypes, each one evolving from its predecessor, with various refinements and modifications based on sea trials. He made his first full size prototype, *Squid 1*, on the first floor of the family home in Hythe where the air could be maintained at a sufficiently high temperature for working with polyester resin. He used his drawings to make a wooden lattice mould which he covered with strips of PVC foam, resin and fiberglass to produce a foam-sandwich construction. An orange pigment was added to the external gel coat to make the boat conspicuous at sea. The hull was then slid through a window, winched down to the garden and taken to the coach house for smoothing off and fitting out.

Gerald also made fibreglass moulds for the hydrofoils. These hydrofoils were connected to the hull with cables and aluminium tubes that fitted into sockets on each side of the cockpit.

Gerald describes in his notes the first sea trial from the beach in Hythe: *'Squid 1 just launched, May 1971. She was almost to scale; the outriggers were closer together and the mast was a little higher. She sailed just like the model and more than twice as fast, but there were problems! She was very easy to launch and beach. Much was learned about rigging and handling this new type of boat by trial and error.'*

Squid 1 was filmed by the BBC sailing in Hythe Bay, in July 1971. I can remember going aboard a fishing boat with the film crew to watch, I must have been four years old at the time. Whistles and shouts of encouragement from the fishermen would reach a crescendo every time my father sped past in his *Foiler*. After a successful sail in the morning, Gerald took one of their crew aboard *Squid 1* with their priceless camera to film from the narrow cockpit.

The BBC also filmed one of the model *Foilers* on the River Hamble for the *Tomorrow's World* television programme. Their presenter, Raymond Baxter, gave the promising remark: *"This little model may prove to be the fastest sailing craft afloat."*

Gerald then designed and built another prototype that incorporated submerged hydrofoils under the bow that could be slid up and down vertically. It was 26ft in length with a 4ft beam and had a slightly flatter curve at the midship cross section. As the boat gained speed it began to rise out of the water. This *Foiler* was entered for the Royal Yachting Association's world speed trials at Weymouth in September 1972 but unfortunately one of the foils was damaged just before the start of the race.

Gerald sailing Squid 2 on the gravel pit lake in Hythe, 1974 ▶

▲ Gerald testing his 26ft Foiler before sailing at Weymouth
▼ Gerald with Squid 2 shortly after landing at Hythe beach, 1974

After two more years of experimentation and thought, Gerald produced another design, *Squid 2*. For practical reasons he abandoned the idea of using submerged foils under the hull. He also devised an innovative construction method whereby strips of foam from a large reel wound off onto a rotating mould. The boat was launched in January 1974. Gerald was pleased with the outcome: '*Squid 2 manoeuvred like a dream and self-steered at an average speed of 17 knots.*' Jack Knights, a correspondent from the *Yachts and Yachting* magazine, went for a sail with Gerald on the gravel pit lake in Hythe aboard *Squid 2,* in July 1974. He came out with these flattering comments: '*After years of experimenting, Mr. Holtom has succeeded in producing a remarkable craft, which if it were produced in a longer version, would stand a good chance of beating the world sailing speed record. The Foiler really is the third sailing alternative after the keel and the multihull.*'

Launching the *Foiler* in the sea at Hythe was always an exciting event for the family and our friends. After the foils, outriggers and mast had been fixed to the hull with cables, the boat would be pushed over the shingle on inflatable rollers. Each time a roller squeezed from the stern somebody would put it back under the bow. Gerald would hold out a wind gauge at arm's length and observe the rise and fall of the disc in the transparent tube that indicated the strength of the wind. If the weather conditions were good the *Foiler* would be pushed into the sea before the next big wave came crashing onto the shingle. The passengers, who would sometimes be Rebecca and myself, would be safely seated in the front cockpit while Gerald scrambled aboard from the stern. The sails would flap and the boat would tilt, with the windward foil poised over the water, as he grabbed the tiller and pulled in the sheets to manoeuvre the *Foiler* out to sea.

The Board of Trade shipped out two factory-made examples of the *Foiler* to represent Britain at the World Fair Marine Expo 75, held in Okinawa in Japan. In 1977 *Foiler Ltd.* manufactured the '*Foiler One-Design*' in Birmingham, based on the lines of *Squid 2*, with patents in Britain, USA, Canada, France and West Germany. They were sold as a hydrofoil day boat: '*Designed for 17 knots and to make possible a more adventurous use of the coastline and the wide open spaces.*'

Gerald's *Foiler* project culminated in the construction of a formidable 52ft hull at a boatyard in Brightlingsea, Essex. It was transported to a piece of land at the back of the Fisherman's Beach in Hythe. Its top speed when finished was expected to be in the region of 40 knots. Gerald had hoped to complete the fitting out for sea trials and possibly a transatlantic crossing, but he was unable to fulfil his dreams. He died on 18 September 1985, at the age of 71. He is buried in Spring Lane Cemetery in Hythe, with two Peace Symbols engraved on his tombstone.

Gerald had once been described as a painter and designer with some of the characteristics of an absent-minded inventor, but when asked if he was an inventor he said: *"I wouldn't have used such a grand word, I am an artist and an artist has to invent all the time, that is his job."*

Epilogue

Designing and making the *Foiler* in Hythe had absorbed Gerald's creative energy and given him emotional release from his involvement with the Aldermaston marches. However, *Women for Life on Earth*, who remained campaigning against nuclear cruise missiles at Greenham Common, would never be far from his thoughts. On his desk there would always be an edition of the CND periodical, *Sanity*, as well as the latest reports from *Greenpeace.*

Gerald was convinced that renewable and safe energy sources could be harnessed from the sun, the wind and the tide to provide all the energy we need. He saw the great potential for developing tidal and wind power in Britain. His ideas led him to experiment with various designs of vertical axis wind turbines that he made and tested in his garden in Hythe.

In the summer of 1972 Gerald travelled with his family to the Languedoc region of southern France, where the Mediterranean landscapes had inspired other artists such as Gustave Courbet. Regular visits were made for many years after, particularly during the summer months. He loved to catch sight of a Bonelli eagle soaring high above the Larzac plateau, or swim in the crystal clear water that flows through the limestone gorges. The glimpse of a green lizard rustling through the undergrowth or the appearance of a hoopoe, with its fine curved beak, would fill him with wonder.

In 2008 I went with my sister Rebecca and both our families to Aldermaston, to commemorate fifty years of protest against the manufacture of nuclear weapons. Looking through the perimeter fence surrounding the Atomic Weapons Research Establishment, as my father had done in 1958, I could see that the buildings were still there. What had changed? Could a revolution of thought take place, from the rule by force of armaments to the concept of non-violence?

Nine countries are now in possession of nuclear weapons: China, France, Britain, the United States of America, India, Pakistan, Israel, North Korea and Russia. Thousands of nuclear missiles have been manufactured, capable of travelling at high speed across oceans and continents, with unimaginable consequences. One missile alone could totally destroy a city the size of London, causing millions of deaths from the explosion and radioactive contamination. The invasion of Ukraine by Russian forces on 24 February 2022, together with the formation of military alliances and the growing tensions between China and the USA over Taiwan, have led us into another Cold War. It has also drawn our attention to a problem that has never been resolved: how to secure peace and eliminate the possibility of a nuclear war? Gerald Holtom was an artist who thought that the answer lies in the responsibility of the individual. As a first step towards peace in the world, he believed in unilateral nuclear disarmament. He created the Peace Symbol to remind us that peace, however difficult it may be to achieve, must be given priority, if life on earth is to be preserved.

LEFT, LEFT, LEFT
A personal account of six protest campaigns 1945-1965

"Peggy Duff is one of the unsung heroes of the struggles for peace and justice in the post-World War II period. She was a founder and leading figure in the Campaign for Nuclear Disarmament, which was instrumental in bringing the dire threat of nuclear war to general attention. Among activists, if not the general public, she is widely recognized – by some (like me) virtually revered – for her incredible contributions to the international movement of protest against the US wars in

Indochina. Peggy was indefatigable, a highly effective organizer, patient and persistent in bringing together the many complex strands of opposition to US crimes in Indochina, the worst of the post-war era. Only those deeply involved were fully aware of this impressive accomplishment, which alone would easily merit the Nobel Peace Prize. And it was far from her only major achievement. The list ranges from her defence of the rights of prisoners of war in the early post-war years to her courageous role in the thankless struggle for Palestinian rights. Truly a remarkable person, and speaking personally, a close and deeply valued friend."

Noam Chomsky

£15 | 308 pages | Paperback | ISBN 9780851248813
www.spokesmanbooks.org